T0235246

Communications
in Computer and Information Science   1736

More information about this series at https://link.springer.com/bookseries/7899

Yi Sun · Liang Cai · Wei Wang · Xianhua Song ·
Zeguang Lu (Eds.)

Blockchain Technology and Application

5th CCF China Blockchain Conference, CBCC 2022
Wuxi, China, December 23–25, 2022
Proceedings

Editors
Yi Sun
Chinese Academy of Sciences
Beijing, China

Wei Wang
Beijing Jiaotong University
Beijing, China

Zeguang Lu
National Academy of Guo Ding Institute
of Data Science
Beijing, China

Liang Cai
Zhejiang University
Hangzhou, China

Xianhua Song
Harbin University of Science and Technology
Harbin, China

ISSN 1865-0929   ISSN 1865-0937 (electronic)
Communications in Computer and Information Science
ISBN 978-981-19-8876-9   ISBN 978-981-19-8877-6 (eBook)
https://doi.org/10.1007/978-981-19-8877-6

This Springer imprint is published by the registered company Springer Nature Singapore Pte Ltd.
The registered company address is: 152 Beach Road, #21-01/04 Gateway East, Singapore 189721, Singapore

Preface

As the program chairs of the 2022 CCF China Blockchain Conference (CBCC 2022), it is our great pleasure to welcome you to the conference proceedings. CBCC 2022 was held in Wuxi, China, during December 23–25, 2022, hosted by the China Computer Federation, the Blockchain Committee of the China Computer Federation, and the National Academy of Sea of Clouds Intelligent Technology Laboratory. The goal of the CBCC conference is to provide a forum for blockchain scientists and engineers.

This year's conference attracted 67 paper submissions. After the hard work of the Program Committee, with each paper receiving at least 3 reviews in a double-blind process, seven papers were accepted to appear in the conference proceedings, giving an acceptance rate of 10.4%. The major topic of this conference was blockchain science and technology.

We would like to thank all the Program Committee members (137 people from 104 different institutes) for their hard work in completing the review tasks. Their collective efforts made it possible to attain quality reviews for all the submissions within a few weeks. Their diverse expertise in different research areas helped us to create an exciting program for the conference. Their comments and advice helped the authors to improve the quality of their papers and gain deeper insights.

Many thanks should also go to the authors and participants for their tremendous support in making the conference a success.

We thank the team at Springer, whose professional assistance was invaluable in the production of the proceedings. A big thanks also to the authors and participants for their tremendous support in making the conference a success.

Besides the technical program, this year CBCC 2022 offered different experiences to the participants. We hope you enjoyed the conference.

November 2022

Yi Sun
Liang Cai

Organization

The 2022 CCF China Blockchain Conference (CBCC 2022), https://conf.ccf.org.cn/CBCC202, was held in Wuxi, China, during December 23–25, 2022, hosted by the China Computer Federation, the Blockchain Committee of the China Computer Federation, and the National Academy of Sea of Clouds Intelligent Technology Laboratory.

General Chairs

Xueming Si   Shanghai Jiao Tong University, China
Dawu Gu   Shanghai Jiao Tong University, China
Liehuang Zhu   Beijing Institute of Technology, China

Program Chairs

Yi Sun   Chinese Academy of Sciences, China
Liang Cai   Zhejiang University, China

Organization Chairs

Yong Ding   Chinese Academy of Sciences, China
Yuan Luo   Guilin University of Electronic Technology, China

Forum Chairs

Jianming Zhu   Central University of Finance and Economics,
                       China
Jun Li   Xiong'an New Area Block Chain Laboratory,
                       China

Publication Chairs

Xianhua Song   Harbin University of Science and Technology,
                       China
Zeguang Lu   National Academy of Guo Ding Institute of Data
                       Science, China

Publicity Chair

Wei Wang   Beijing Jiao Tong University, China

Program Committee

Hongzhang An   The 30th Research Institute of China Electronics
                                   Technology Corporation, China
Mingjun Cai   Beijing Touken Technology Co., Ltd., China
Hengjin Cai   Wuhan University, China
Chunjie Cao   Hainan University, China
Yuan Cao   Hunan Chenhan Information Technology Co.,
                                   Ltd., China
Dynasty Cao   Huawei Technologies Co., Ltd., China
Hall Chen   University of Electronic Science and Technology,
                                   China
Jing Chen   Wuhan University, China
Jianhai Chen   Zhejiang University, China
Laizhong Cui   Shenzhen University, China
Xiaohui Cui   Wuhan University, China
Bingrong Dai   Shanghai Computer Software Technology
                                   Development Center, China
Yong Ding   Guilin University of Electronic Science and
                                   Technology, China
Xuewen Dong   Xi'an University of Electronic Science and
                                   Technology, China
Li Duan   Beijing Jiao Tong University, China
Yongkai Fan   Communication University of China, China
Dawn Fang   Nanjing University of Aeronautics and
                                   Astronautics, China
Shaojing Fu   National University of Defense Technology,
                                   China
Zhangjie Fu   Nanjing University of Information Engineering,
                                   China
Zhipeng Gao   Beijing University of Posts and
                                   Telecommunications, China
Jianbin Gao   University of Electronic Science and Technology,
                                   China
Chengshi Gao   Shanghai Hashi Information Technology
                                   Partnership, China
Sheng Gao   Central University of Finance and Economics,
                                   China
Dawu Gu   Shanghai Jiao Tong University, China
Zhitao Guan   North China Electric Power University, China

Xiaobing Guo	Lenovo Research, China
Weili Han	Fudan University, China
Yukun Hao	Shanghai Wanxiang Blockchain Co., Ltd., China
Yunhua He	Northern Polytechnic University, China
Haiwu He	Beijing Hualian European Chain Network Technology Co., Ltd., China
Guangyu He	Neusoft Group Co., Ltd., China
Daojing He	Harbin University of Technology, Shenzhen, China
Chao He	Huawei Technologies Co., Ltd., China
Debiao He	Wuhan University, China
Chunqiang Hu	Chongqing University, China
Butian Huang	Hangzhou Yunxiang Network Technology Co., Ltd., China
Jianhua Huang	East China University of Science and Technology, China
Huawei Huang	Sun Yat-sen University, China
Chengchen Ji	Shenzhen Zhongxiang Internet Technology Co., Ltd., China
Shouling Ji	Zhejiang University, China
Daming Jia	Xindao Technology Co., Ltd., China
Yu Jiang	Guangzhou University, China
Xinwen Jiang	Xiangtan University, China
Cheqing Jin	East China Normal University, China
Weipeng Jing	Northeast Forestry University, China
Haibin Kan	Fudan University, China
Lanju Kong	Shandong University, China
Kai Lei	Peking University Shenzhen Graduate School, China
Wei Li	Peking University Shenzhen Graduate School, China
Chao Li	Beijing Jiao Tong University, China
Yong Li	Beijing Jiao Tong University, China
Zhuo Li	Daofu Information Technology (Zhejiang) Co., Ltd., China
Qilei Li	Hangzhou Production Chain Digital Technology Co., Ltd., China
Wei Li	Hangzhou Qulian Technology Co., Ltd., China
Meng Li	Hefei Polytechnic University, China
Xuelei Li	Inspur (Beijing) Electronic Information Industry Co., Ltd., China
Lizhong Li	Lizhan Group, China
Guangshun Li	Qufu Normal University, China

Tianrui Li	Southwest Jiao Tong University, China
Jun Li	Xiong'an New Area Block Chain Laboratory, China
Ming Li	China Electronics Technology Standardization Institute, China
Xuedong Liang	Sichuan University, China
Xiubo Liang	Zhejiang University, China
Shaofu Lin	Beijing University of Technology, China
Changlu Lin	Fujian Normal University, China
Wenyin Liu	Guangdong University of Technology, China
Yuan Liu	Guangzhou University, China
Yang Liu	Henan University of Technology, China
Baixiang Liu	Fudan University, China
Xiulong Liu	Tianjin University, China
Xiaofan Liu	City University of Hong Kong, Hong Kong, China
Tiancheng Liu	Easy to see Supply Chain Management Co., Ltd., China
Zhenguang Liu	Zhejiang Gongshang University, China
Chengnian Long	Shanghai Jiao Tong University, China
Yuan Luo	Shanghai Jiao Tong University, China
Min Luo	Wuhan University, China
Hongliang Mao	National Internet Emergency Center, China
Hongwei Meng	Xiong'an New Area Block Chain Laboratory, China
Baoning Niu	Taiyuan University of Technology, China
Anqun Pan	Tencent, China
Heng Pan	Zhongyuan University of Technology, China
Binbing Qian	PLA Marine Environment Special Office, China
Qiang Qu	Shenzhen Advanced Technology Research Institute, Chinese Academy of Sciences, China
Yanli Ren	Shanghai University, China
Na Ruan	Shanghai Jiao Tong University, China
Zhou Shao	Asian Infrastructure Investment Bank, China
Meng Shen	Beijing University of Technology, China
Yulong Shen	Xi'an University of Electronic Science and Technology, China
Xingguo Shi	Suzhou Chao Blockchain Information Technology Co., Ltd., China
Yuan Su	Shaanxi Lidai Operational Research Information Technology Co., Ltd., China
Yi Sun	Institute of Computing Technology, Chinese Academy of Sciences, China

Xiaoming Sun	Institute of Computing Technology, Chinese Academy of Sciences, China
Zhiyong Tan	Beijing Oulian Technology Co., Ltd., China
Huanming Tan	Fujian Fulian Technology Co., Ltd., China
Hua Tang	South China Normal University, China
Youliang Tian	Guizhou University, China
Hui Tian	Overseas Chinese University, China
Zhiguo Wan	Zhijiang Laboratory, China
Wei Wang	Beijing Jiao Tong University, China
Licheng Wang	Beijing University of Posts and Telecommunications, China
Jing Wang	Bubi (Beijing) Network Technology Co., Ltd., China
Liangmin Wang	Jiangsu University, China
Lianhai Wang	Shandong Computing Center, China
Hao Wang	Shandong Normal University, China
Jinsong Wang	Tianjin University of Technology, China
Yichuan Wang	Xi'an University of Technology, China
Yazhe Wang	Institute of Information Engineering, Chinese Academy of Sciences, China
Songjie Wei	Nanjing University of Technology, China
Yihong Wen	The 54th Research Institute of China Electronics Technology Corporation, China
Qianhong Wu	Beijing University of Aeronautics and Astronautics, China
Bin Wu	Institute of Information Engineering, Chinese Academy of Sciences, China
Guangjun Wu	Institute of Information Engineering, Chinese Academy of Sciences, China
Qi Xia	University of Electronic Science and Technology, China
Tao Xiang	Chongqing University, China
Jiang Xiao	Huazhong University of Science and Technology, China
Wei Xie	Loudi Wanbao New Area Development and Investment Group Co., Ltd., China
Yong Xie	Qinghai University, China
Chunxiao Xing	Tsinghua University, China
Guangxia Xu	Guangzhou University, China
Yang Xu	Hunan University, China
Haixia Xu	Institute of Information Engineering, Chinese Academy of Sciences, China

Kaiping Xue	China University of Science and Technology, China
Yong Yan	State Grid Zhejiang Electric Power Co., Ltd., China
Ying Yan	Ant Gold Clothes, China
Yang Yang	Fuzhou University, China
Zheng Yang	Hunan Tianhe Guoyun Technology Co., Ltd., China
Yang Yang	Shenzhen Block Continental Technology Co., Ltd., China
Dong Yang	Renmin University of China, China
Su Yao	Tsinghua University, China
Keting Yin	Zhejiang University, China
Lei Yu	Institute of Computing Technology, Chinese Academy of Sciences, China
Jianing Yu	Blockchain Special Committee of China Communications Industry Association, China
Zhiwei Zhang	Beijing University of Technology, China
Yuchao Zhang	Beijing University of Posts and Telecommunications, China
Shibin Zhang	Chengdu University of Information Engineering, China
Yin Zhang	University of Electronic Science and Technology, China
Lejun Zhang	Guangzhou University, China
Yifeng Zhang	Hangzhou Blockchain Technology Research Institute, China
Xiang Zhang	Huawei Technologies Co., Ltd., China
Jun Zhang	Inner Mongolia University, China
Yan Zhang	University of Oslo, Norway
Hongwei Zhang	Tianjin University of Technology, China
Zhihong Zhang	Zhengzhou University, China
Rui Zhang	Institute of Information Engineering, Chinese Academy of Sciences, China
Qinglin Zhao	Macao University of Science and Technology, Macao, China
Yunlei Zhao	Fudan University, China
Huawei Zhao	Qilu University of Technology, China
Fan Zhao	Xinjiang Institute of Physical and Chemical Technology, Chinese Academy of Sciences, China
Hong Zheng	East China University of Science and Technology, China

Contents

A Proxy Re-encryption Scheme of Medical Data Sharing Based on Consortium Blockchain

Juxia Li, Xing Zhang(✉), and Zhiguang Chu

Liaoning University of Technology, Jinzhou 121001, Liaoning, China
209807029@stu.lnut.edu.cn

Abstract. In order to solve the problem of sharing medical data among different hospitals, this paper proposes a multi-party secure sharing scheme of medical information based on a consortium blockchain. Based on proxy re-encryption technology and user identity attributes, the scheme divides the permissions of data users in fine granularity, and solves the problems of data tracking and access control, uses cloud computing to store medical data, reduces the capital investment of hospital hardware equipment, reduces maintenance costs, and uses NTRU encryption technology to ensure the anonymity and anti-collusion security of medical data. Using Federation chains to store and record data operations ensures the safe sharing of data. The performance evaluation results show that the proposed re-encryption scheme for shared medical data agents based on a consortium blockchain has higher superiority in data protection, privacy security, rights allocation, etc. Compared with blockchain work in recent years, the result shows that the scheme has certain superiority. The purpose of this scheme is to provide new ideas for the safe sharing of medical data in the future.

Keywords: Blockchain · Identity based proxy re-encryption · Authority access control · NTRU encryption · Cloud storage

1 Introduction

With the development of information technology, people's access to information is gradually diversified. At the same time, the risk of privacy disclosure is also greatly increased. The problem of Information Island in the medical field and the security of medical data have attracted much attention [1]. In his (hospital information system), the patient's electronic medical record contains the patient's basic information, which is mainly managed by medical institutions. Relevant laws and regulations have strict restrictions and regulations on the transmission of private data, which makes the patient's diagnosis and treatment data scattered in different storage areas and can't be shared, resulting in the phenomenon of information island, it leads to waste of resources and reduces the interoperability between hospitals. The collection of medical big data can be used for medical research and research and the development of medical equipment, which has great social and commercial value. However, this information involves patients' privacy and security. How to ensure the security of medical data is an urgent problem to be solved.

© The Author(s), under exclusive license to Springer Nature Singapore Pte Ltd. 2022
Y. Sun et al. (Eds.): CBCC 2022, CCIS 1736, pp. 1–12, 2022.
https://doi.org/10.1007/978-981-19-8877-6_1

The growing maturity of blockchain technology makes data sharing between medical institutions possible. It gets rid of traditional third-party tools, does not rely on specific central nodes, realizes P2P transactions, and avoids the risk of privacy disclosure caused by a single point of failure. The tamper-proof, decentralization, and traceability of blockchain provide good conditions for the storage of medical data. In the process of data upload, the identity-based authority proxy re-encryption technology is used to control the range of medical data that visitors can view through the authorization granted by patients to visitors of different levels. Therefore, this paper proposes a shared medical data proxy re-encryption scheme based on the consortium blockchain. Each medical institution acts as a single node and each medical institution forms a consortium blockchain. Only the institutions in the consortium blockchain can maintain the data in the blockchain, and other unauthorized nodes have no access [2]. Patients in the medical institution are responsible for uploading medical data and setting hospital access permissions, when the hospital sends a request for calling information, if the access right of the hospital is in the allowable access data set by the patient, the proxy server re-encrypts the data and the hospital completes the download.

2 Preliminary

2.1 Blockchain Technology

Blockchain originated from bitcoin, and then there have been alternative currencies with better privacy protection effects such as Dascoin, Monroe coin, and Zcash. It is a decentralized storage technology based on P2P network architecture. It was first described in 2008 [3]. A special information transmission mechanism was adopted between nodes in the mode of relay forwarding, gradually the information to the whole domain. It abandons the traditional trusteeship service relying on a reliable third party, supports point-to-point whole process anonymous transactions, greatly reduces the risk of network eavesdropping, and effectively protects the user's information security.

Working Principle. The blockchain system is composed of a block header, block body, and policy header, which form a sequential chain structure in the form of "series". The block header encapsulates the version number, previous block hash value, timestamp, random value, and Merkle root. The number of transactions is recorded in the block body. Except for the creation block, each block in the blockchain contains the hash value of the previous block [1]; Fig. 1 shows the specific structure of the blockchain. The workflow is as follows:

1. The node uploads the encrypted transaction information and broadcasts it to the nodes of the whole network in the form of relay forwarding.
2. The miner performs signature verification on the collected transaction information and writes the valid information into the block.
3. The transaction information in a period of time is formed into a new candidate block, and the node obtains the workload proof meeting the target difficulty through the PoW consensus mechanism.
4. Broadcast the blocks found by this node to the whole network.

5. The whole network node verifies this node. When the transaction information is valid and has never existed, it passes the verification, adds it to the blockchain, and creates a new blockchain behind this block.

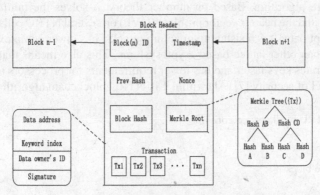

Fig. 1. Block structure

Consensus Algorithm. The consensus algorithm was originally used to study the traditional distributed data consistency problem. In 1982, Lamport proposed the "Byzantine general problem" to study how to make all nodes reach a consensus when there are dishonest nodes in the network. Aiming at this problem, Lamport first proposed the Byzantine fault tolerance (BFT) algorithm. In 1999, Castro et al. Proposed practical Byzantine fault tolerance (PBFT), that is, when the dishonest nodes in the network are less than 1/3 of the nodes in the whole network, the whole network can reach a consensus. Compared with the BFT algorithm, the complexity of the PBFT algorithm is greatly reduced, Reduce waste of arithmetic and power. In 1993, Cynthia proposed the concept of PoW (proof of work, PoW). Then, Nakamoto announced that bitcoin uses the PoW consensus mechanism, which relies on strong computing power to ensure the security and non-tamperability of the blockchain. If you want to tamper with the data in the block, you need to master more than 51% of the computing power of the whole network, it ensures the security of the transaction [4].

In 2012, peer coin adopted the proof of stake (POS) mechanism as the consensus mechanism and selected the node with the highest interest in the system for bookkeeping according to the currency age. Compared with the PoW consensus, it improved the transaction efficiency and increased the throughput. In 2014, Dan proposed the delegated proof of steady (DPoS), which is similar to the "Board of directors", the members of the "board of directors" are elected by democratic election. The members need to pay a certain deposit and can get benefit from the transaction fees. The consensus mechanism ensures the interests of nodes, speeds up the block out speed, and can realize rapid consensus verification [5].

2.2 NTRU Encryption Algorithm

The NTRU (Number Theory Research Unit) algorithm is a public key system [6] invented in 1996 by three American math professors (Jeffrey Hoffstein, Jill Pipher, and Joseph H.Silverman). The NTRU algorithm is divided into NTRU encryption algorithm and NTRU signature algorithm. Based on number theory, it solves the minimum vector problem (SVP) and the nearest vector problem (CVP) on several NTRU cells to generate keys and decrypt data. It is resistant to quantum attacks, has lower complexity and less storage space than other lattice-based cryptosystems. This also means that the NTRU algorithm generates keys faster and has lower requirements for processors and memory at the same level of security [7]. Algorithm 1 is NTRU blockchain algorithm.

Algorithm1: NTRU blockchain algorithm
Case1
if new block
NTRU signature block
end if
If relay broadcast to each block
Blockchain consensus
Add a new block to blockchain
End if
Case 2
If no consensus
don't add new block
End if

2.3 Identity-Based Proxy Re-encryption Technology

Identity-based proxy re-encryption was originally proposed by Green and Ateniese [8]. This extends the proxy re-encryption technology to an authentication-based system. It does not require public key certificates and certificate management systems, authenticates the user's identity information, and generates the user's private key using the private key generator (PKG). This completes the conversion of Alice's encrypted data to Bob can decrypt [9]. With IB-PRE technology, encrypted data can be transmitted to different users and different keys can be generated to decrypt the data without using the shared public key as an intermediate link, which not only increases the security of the information but also reduces the complexity of the operation.

3 Security Sharing of Medical Data

3.1 Scheme System Description

This model contains two entity models: hospital, patient. It uses P2P technology, consensus technology, NTRU encryption algorithm, identity-based agent re-encryption technology, and smart contract to ensure the secure storage and sharing of information.

- **Grade Decision Center (GDC).** GDC is a trusted third party and authoritative. Patients and hospital organizations need to complete the identity registration in GDC. GDC receives the identity ID information and returns the identity level information G and private key SKID. When patients upload the electronic medical record information, the self-level G returned by GDC is embedded in the encrypted electronic medical record ET, Encrypt (P, E, G) → ET. The Hierarchy Decision Center embeds the user access condition set C into the re-encrypted key RKID and uploads it to the proxy server, P is the public key for identity information and E is the electronic medical record information [10]. When $G \in C$, the user information {ID, RKID} is uploaded and the ET is re-encrypted by the proxy server. Conversely, the re-encryption operation cannot be performed. The medical data is encrypted and uploaded to the proxy server. The proxy server encrypts the information to the cloud storage using NTRU cryptography. The blockchain layer records the operations performed in the cloud. Once the information is recorded by the blockchain system, it cannot be tampered with or deleted.
- **Patient.** The patient uses the public key P to encrypt the electronic medical record, embeds the identity level G in the electronic medical record, and uploads it to the proxy server.
- **Hospital.** The hospital sends a download request to the proxy server. If the hospital has the right to download the document, $G \in C$, it can download the ciphertext and decrypt the ETID with the hospital's private key SKID.
- **Proxy server (PS).** After the PS receives the download request from the user, it determines the user's permission. If $G \in C$, it re-encrypts the ciphertext. Conversely, rejects the user's download request.
- **Cloud computing.** Encrypted documents on cloud storage servers.
- **Consortium blockchain.** The blockchain records the upload, download, and other operations of data in the cloud. Once the data is recorded in the blockchain, it will not be tampered with, which effectively ensures the privacy and security of patients, and can also effectively monitor the data transmission process [11].

Taking hospitals as nodes, multiple hospitals jointly form a consortium blockchain and use the consensus mechanism of blockchain to synchronize information between blockchains, it improves the efficiency of Cross hospital treatment, shortens the medical time, and saves time and economic cost. Table 1 explains the English words abbreviated in the text.

In this scheme, information sharing between patients and hospitals and between hospitals can be ensured. In the process of information transmission, patients have absolute control and use rights over their medical information. Through the fine-grained division of access rights, the hospital is granted the information range of electronic medical records. The information is allowed to be called only after permission is obtained, it ensures the security and privacy of data. This scheme makes use of the characteristics of NTRU lattice, such as low complexity, resistance to quantum attacks, and smaller storage space, and encrypts the data in the cloud for secondary storage. Even if the data is leaked in any transmission process, the data receiver will get the encrypted data, but can't obtain the corresponding private key SK_{ID} cracking data, which fully protects the security of the patient's medical data, it provides a double guarantee for multi-party data security sharing.

Table 1. Notation

Symbol	Meaning
ET	Chipertext
Patient	Data owner
Hospital	Data user
GDC	Grade decision center
G	Identity level
C	Access condition-set
SK_{ID}	Private key
RK_{ID}	Re-encryption key

3.2   Identity-Based Hierarchical Re-encryption Process

The proposed scheme model is shown in Fig. 2. The scheme includes Federation chains for data sharing between hospitals and identity-based rights agent re-encryption technology [9], which is used for sharing and encrypting medical data. Identity-based privilege re-encryption technology is used to encrypt patients' medical data. During the encryption process, fine-grained user privileges, and corresponding access privileges are granted by the user level G. The specific steps are as follows:

1. Join the Grade Decision Center (GDC), which is a trusted third party and authoritative. The patients and hospitals register their identity information with GDC. GDC returns the corresponding private key SK_{ID} and identity level information G to the registrant based on the identity information and GDC uploads the re-encrypted secret key of the user's identity to the proxy server.
2. The patient encrypts the electronic medical record with the public key P of the identity information, embeds the grade information G, obtains the ciphertext ET, and uploads the ET to the proxy server.
3. The proxy server encrypts the documents with NTRU encryption and uploads them to the cloud.
4. Federation chains record each operation of cloud data, and once the data is recorded, it cannot be deleted or tampered with.
5. Hospitals send download requests to the cloud. If identity level information G is in the condition set C accessed by users, servers work with encryption cards to convert ciphertext into re-encrypted data that can be decrypted by hospitals using private keys, and the download is completed [12].

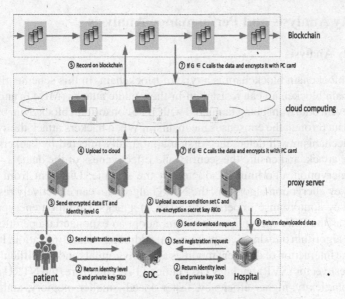

Fig. 2. Data security sharing system model

3.3 Consortium Blockchain Medical Data Sharing Process

The medical data-sharing consortium blockchain is composed of multiple hospitals. Each hospital as a single node of the blockchain encrypts and uploads the ciphertext ET to the consortium blockchain with NTRU cryptosystem [13], which can provide multiple protections for patients' privacy. In this consortium blockchain, hospitals can share medical data by using the consensus mechanism of blockchain. The specific steps are as follows:

1. The patient encrypts his medical information, embeds the grade information G, and uploads the encrypted information to the proxy server.
2. The proxy server uses NTRU system encryption to synchronize the information on the consortium blockchain blockchain.
3. When patients are seeking medical treatment across hospitals, the GDC reauthorizes them, grants access to hospital records on the Federation chain, and the hospital obtains medical information from patients in other hospitals.
4. Complete information sharing.

4 Security Analysis and Performance Analysis

4.1 Security Analysis

Consortium blockchain blockchain is a type of blockchain. In this scheme, the consortium blockchain blockchain can resist man-in-the-middle attacks (MIMT) and anomaly attacks to prevent data from being tampered with. The consortium blockchain blockchain verifies the data through the consensus mechanism. When hackers attack the system, the consensus mechanism will detect the version abnormally injected by hackers, identify and resist the attack, and ensure the security and effectiveness of the data.

NTRU encryption algorithm is adopted in the scheme. Different from the common public-key encryption algorithm, the NTRU algorithm can effectively resist replay attacks and key compromise impersonation (KCI) attacks. Common encryption algorithms, such as the RSA encryption algorithm, adopt an exponential operation mechanism. NTRU algorithm only involves polynomial addition and multiplication. Its security is based on the interaction of different modules and polynomials and the difficulty of finding the shortest.vector (SVP) on the NTRU lattice [14]. Therefore, the NTRU algorithm has lower complexity, higher efficiency, faster speed, smaller memory, and relatively low requirements for a processor. Table 2 shows several groups of standard parameters recommended by NTRU.

Table 2. NTRU standard parameters

Safety level	N	p	q	D_j	D_r	D_g	c	Decoding time (year)
Excellent	503	3	256	216	55	72	0.18	$\approx 62 \times 10^{27}$
Middle	167	3	128	61	18	20	0.23	≈ 380
Common	107	3	64	15	5	12	0.2582	≈ 0.025

The identity-based authority proxy re-encryption technology does not share the public key, which reduces the risk of data disclosure. At the same time, through the fine-grained division of user authority, it achieves the purpose of hierarchical data management and Hierarchical Authorization. Users of different levels can see the data of the corresponding level. According to patients' wishes, protect patients' privacy and safety reasonably and effectively.

4.2 Performance Analysis

In this scheme, the patient only needs to encrypt the data once, and the hospital only needs to decrypt the data once. Compared with the traditional proxy re-encryption scheme, neither patient nor hospital needs to participate in agent re-encrypted key generation, which improves the efficiency of data upload and download, reduces the amount of additional calculation, and saves the time cost.

In the process of data cloud storage, the NTRU cryptosystem is selected for secondary encryption. In this scheme, three public keys with different lengths are selected according to the NTRU security level for a comparative experiment. Their secret key lengths are 167 bytes, 263 bytes, and 503 bytes, respectively. The security of 167 bytes, 263 bytes and 503 bytes of the NTRU cryptosystem is at least equivalent to that of 512 bytes, 1024 bytes and 2048 bytes of RSA encryption algorithm and 108 bytes, 163 bytes and 210 bytes of the ECC algorithm. In order to verify the superiority of the NTRU algorithm, we have carried out encryption and decryption experiments on three groups of data respectively. Figure 3 and Fig. 4 are the experimental results. The experimental results show that under the same security level, the number of information blocks encrypted by the NTRU algorithm per second is much more than that encrypted by the RSA algorithm and the ECC algorithm. During decryption, the decryption time of the RSA algorithm is the longest and that of the NTRU algorithm is the shortest. According on the experimental comparison, NTRU cryptography is better than RSA and ECC cryptography.

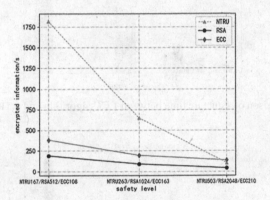

Fig. 3. Number of information blocks encrypted by NTRU, RSA and ECC per second

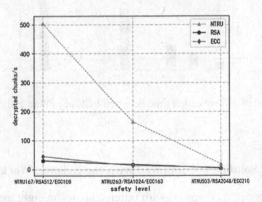

Fig. 4. Number of information blocks decrypted by NTRU, RSA and ECC per second

The results in Figs. 3 and 4 show that the RSA algorithm is less efficient than the ECC and NTRU algorithms in encrypting and decrypting information, so it is possible to compare the ECC and NTRU algorithms to determine which one is more appropriate for blockchain. Figure 5 shows the time required for ECC and NTRU algorithms to sign on a block chain at the same level of security. Figure 6 shows the time required for ECC and NTRU algorithms to authenticate on the block chain at the same security level. The experimental results show that NTRU algorithm has higher security level and faster signing and authentication speed on block chains at the same security level.

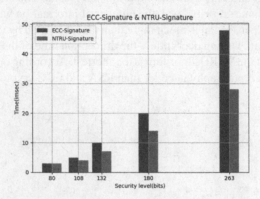

Fig. 5. Comparison of signature time between ECC algorithm and NTRU algorithm

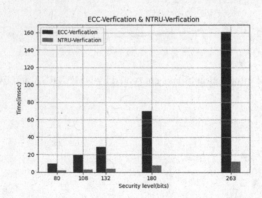

Fig. 6. Comparison of authentication time between ECC algorithm and NTRU algorithm

4.3 The Proposed Solution is Compared with the Existing Work

The scheme in this paper is compared with other schemes in eight aspects: whether the NTRU algorithm is adopted, whether proxy re-encryption technology is adopted, and whether cloud storage is adopted. The results are shown in Table 3, where "$\sqrt{}$" means "yes" and "–" means "no".

Table 3. Comparison between the proposed scheme and the existing scheme

	Ref. [7] (2021)	Ref. [9] (2021)	Ref. [12] (2021)	Ref. [15] (2021)	Ref. [11] (2021)	Ref. [16] (2021)	Ref. [17] (2020)	Our proposal
NTRU algorithm	√	√	–	–	–	–	–	√
Re-encryption	–	√	√	√	–	√	√	√
Cloud architecture	√	√	–	√	–	–	√	√
Alliance chain	–	–	–	–	–	–	–	√
Fine grained	–	–	√	–	–	–	–	√
Smart contract	√	–	–	√	√	√	√	√
Privacy security	√	–	–	√	√	√	√	√
Information multi-party security sharing	–	–	–	–	–	–	–	√

Comparing the proposed scheme with the existing scheme, the comparison results show that none of the existing schemes includes the eight aspects listed in the table. Table 3 shows that the proposed scheme has higher privacy protection, low computing overhead, high efficiency, and hierarchical permission management, which can ensure the secure sharing of information among multiple parties.

5 Conclusion

With the development of information technology, information leakage occurs from time to time in the process of information sharing, which threatens people's privacy and security. Medical information security sharing has become an urgent problem to be solved. To solve this problem, the consortium blockchain blockchain and identity-based authority agent re-encryption technology are adopted in this scheme to fully ensure the patient's information security and realize the multi-party information security sharing between patients and hospitals, hospitals, and hospitals. It is a very promising scheme.

References

1. Wang, H., Zhou, M.: Secure storage model of medical information based on blockchain. Comput. Sci. **46**(12), 174–179 (2019)
2. Zhu, L., et al.: Overview of blockchain privacy protection research. Comput. Res. Dev. **54**(10), 2170–2186 (2017)

3. Hoy, M.B.: An introduction to the blockchain and its implications for libraries and medicine. Med. Reference Serv. Q. **36**(3), 273–279 (2017)
4. Guo, S., Wang, R., Zhang, F.: Overview of the principle and application of blockchain technology. Comput. Sci. **48**(02), 271–281 (2021)
5. Yuan, Y., Wang, F.: Development status and Prospect of blockchain technology. J. Autom. **42**(04), 481–494 (2016)
6. Chen, K., Xie, K.: Analysis of NTRU algorithm. Comput. Eng. (S1), 308–309+322 (2004)
7. Lv, Z., Qiao, L., Hossain, M.S., et al.: Analysis of using blockchain to protect the privacy of drone big data. IEEE Netw. **35**(1), 44–49 (2021)
8. Green, M., Ateniese, G.: Identity-based proxy re-encryption. In: Katz, J., Yung, M. (eds.) ACNS 2007. LNCS, vol. 4521, pp. 288–306. Springer, Heidelberg (2007). https://doi.org/10.1007/978-3-540-72738-5_19
9. Yue, N., Wang, Y., Wang, M.: Identity-based proxy re-encryption over NTRU lattices for cloud computing. Proc. Comput. Sci. **187**, 264–269 (2021)
10. Niu, S., Chen, L., Liu, W.: Attribute-based keyword search encryption scheme with verifiable ciphertext via blockchains. In: 2020 IEEE 9th Joint International Information Technology and Artificial Intelligence Conference (ITAIC), pp. 849–853 (2020). https://doi.org/10.1109/ITAIC49862.2020.9338962
11. Mishra, R.A., Kalla, A., Braeken, A., et al.: Privacy protected blockchain based architecture and implementation for sharing of students' credentials. Inf. Process. Manage. **58**(3), 102512 (2021)
12. Li, L., Yang, H., Dong, X.: File hierarchical access control scheme based on identity multi condition proxy re encryption. Comput. Appl. 1–8 (2021). https://kns-cnki-net.wvpn.lnut.edu.cn/kcms/detail/51.1307.TP.20210831.1704.035.html
13. Natanzi, S.B.H., Majma, M.R.: Secure northbound interface for SDN applications with NTRU public key infrastructure. In: 2017 IEEE 4th International Conference on Knowledge-Based Engineering and Innovation (KBEI), pp. 0452–0458. IEEE (2017)
14. Jeong, S., Park, K.S., Park, Y.H., Park, Y.H.: An efficient NTRU-based authentication protocol in IoT environment. In: Arai, K., Kapoor, S., Bhatia, R. (eds.) SAI 2018. AISC, vol. 857, pp. 1262–1268. Springer, Cham (2019). https://doi.org/10.1007/978-3-030-01177-2_91
15. Manzoor, A., Braeken, A., Kanhere, S.S., et al.: Proxy re-encryption enabled secure and anonymous IoT data sharing platform based on blockchain. J. Netw. Comput. Appl. **176**, 102917 (2021)
16. Agyekum, K.O.-B.O., Xia, Q., Sifah, E.B., Cobblah, C.N.A., Xia, H., Gao, J.: A proxy re-encryption approach to secure data sharing in the internet of things based on blockchain. IEEE Syst. J. (2021). https://doi.org/10.1109/JSYST.2021.3076759
17. Lei, Y., Jia, Z., Yang, Y., Cheng, Y., Fu, J.: A cloud data access authorization update scheme based on blockchain. In: 2020 3rd International Conference on Smart BlockChain (SmartBlock), pp. 33–38 (2020). https://doi.org/10.1109/SmartBlock52591.2020.00014

A Leadership Transfer Algorithm for the Raft

Ruowen Gu and Dongyan Huang[✉]

Guangxi Key Laboratory of Wireless Wideband Communication and Signal Processing, Guilin
University of Electronic Technology, Guilin 541004, Guangxi, China
huangdongyan-gua@163.com

Abstract. The Raft álgorithm is widely used as a consensus algorithm for a private
blockchain. However, the followers in the Raft may fail to continuously receive
heartbeats and become faulty nodes because of unreliable transmission. Faulty
nodes seriously affect consensus efficiency, even causing the network split. The
leader cannot receive enough replies during the network split, so the cluster cannot
reach a consensus for transactions. To improve the efficiency and stability of the
Raft, first, we use the LWLR (Local Weighted Linear Regression) algorithm to
predict the time that a follower becomes a faulty node due to the heartbeat loss
rate, thereby predicting the node states. Then, we update the network split probability model and propose a leadership transfer algorithm to prevent the network
split by replacing the leader. And a leader selection algorithm is also designed to
select the next leader based on a reputation model that evaluates the followers'
stability. Finally, we demonstrate that the predicted node failure time is accurate
by analyzing the error. And we compare the TPS (Transactions Per Second) of the
original Raft and the TPS of the Raft with the leadership transfer algorithm. The
experiment results show that: 1) the predicted node failure time is relatively accurate, which is about 85.7%. 2) The leadership transfer algorithm can considerably
improve the TPS by approximately 500 times compared to the original Raft when
the number of faulty nodes is half of the network size.

Keywords: Blockchain · The heartbeat loss rate · The leadership transfer
algorithm · The LWLR algorithm · The Raft · The network split · The reputation
model

1 Introduction

Blockchain is the underlying technology of Bitcoin [1]. In essence, it's a distributed
database based on a P2P (peer-to-peer) network and cryptography. It can resolve information asymmetry and achieve trust and concerted action between multiple nodes. The

Supported by the Guangxi Key Research and Development Program under Grant AB20238026;
The Guangxi Natural Science Foundation for Youths under Grant 2022GXNSFBA035645; The
Chinese NSF Project under Grant 6217070229; The Director Fund of Key Laboratory of Cog-
nitive Radio and Information Processing, Ministry of Education (Guilin University of Electronic
Technology) under Grant CRKL210104; The Innovation Project of GUET Graduate Education
under Grant 2022YCXS052 and Grant 2021YCXS042.

Y. Sun et al. (Eds.): CBCC 2022, CCIS 1736, pp. 13–30, 2022.
https://doi.org/10.1007/978-981-19-8877-6_2

consensus algorithm is a critical technology that decides the blockchain's QoS (Quality of Service).

Diego Ongaro proposed the Raft algorithm [2] in 2014. Since data only flows from the leader to the followers, the Raft algorithm has a simpler structure and higher consensus efficiency. When the number of faulty nodes is less than half of the network size, it can run normally.

A large amount of research is conducted on the Raft algorithm, with a focus on the analysis and improvement of the performance.

Robert et al. [3] and Philip et al. [4] indicated that the leader's load or delay is too high because all client requests are handled by the leader. So, the leader may not be able to send the heartbeats on time. Ermin et al. [5] used SDN (Software Defined Network) to improve the consistent response time of the Raft algorithm. Christian et al. [6] proposed a new timeout strategy by studying how the node's failure affects the running time of leader election. To optimize the byzantine fault tolerance of the Raft algorithm, Tian et al. [7] proposed a byzantine fault-tolerant algorithm B-Raft combined with the Schnorr signature mechanism. Wang et al. [8] proposed a high-throughput, high-scalability no byzantine fault tolerance algorithm–KRaft to optimize leader election and the consensus process of the Raft algorithm. Pâris et al. [9] proposed a lightweight and dynamic version of the Raft algorithm to reduce energy consumption by changing the arbitration based on the number of available participants. Min et al. [10] introduced a new state-"Favorite" in the Raft algorithm to avoid the unavailability of the system due to the leader downtime., Huang et al. [11] proposed an RBFT algorithm with supervision nodes based on the concept of network slicing, which has byzantine fault tolerance and higher consensus efficiency. Gao et al. [12] proposed the T-PBFT algorithm based on the EigenTrust model, which enhances the robustness by evaluating node trust and constructing a primary group.

Huang et al. [13] were first concerned with the stability of the Raft algorithm. They emphasized that the heartbeat loss rate is the main cause of the nodes failing and the network splitting. Especially for blockchain systems deployed in a wireless environment [14], there is a non-negligible heartbeat loss rate between the leader and the followers. Such as the charging station transaction system based on blockchain [15], and the double incentive energy trading system for the IoT (Internet of Things) and blockchain [16].

Network split is a problem that must be addressed in distributed systems. The network is divided into independent subnetworks for various reasons, and the data is scattered in these disconnected areas. In the Raft algorithm, the cluster after the network split cannot complete the consensus, severely affecting the availability of the clusters.

Assume that the network size is N, the number of faulty nodes is f, and the fault tolerance of the Raft algorithm is $f = (N - 1)/2$. However, faulty nodes greatly affect consensus efficiency. When $f > (N - 1)/2$, the network is split, and the Raft algorithm cannot reach a consensus. Therefore, knowing the node states and preventing the network split are effective methods for improving the Raft algorithm's consensus efficiency and stability.

In this paper, we explore methods to improve the consensus efficiency and stability of the Raft algorithm by predicting the node states to avoid the network split. The main contributions are as follows:

1. We propose a leadership transfer algorithm that actively changes the current leader when the network is facing a split, which prevents the network from splitting.
2. The LWLR algorithm was used to predict the node states by predicting the time that a follower becomes a candidate due to continuously losing heartbeats.
3. We update the network split probability model to find an appropriate time for starting the leadership transfer. It can predict the network split probability based on the number of faulty nodes and the heartbeat loss rate of the followers.
4. We develop a leader selection algorithm based on a reputation model. The follower's stability is evaluated by its load, delay, the number of lost heartbeats, and the logs index, and the next leader is selected according to their reputation value.

The remainder of this paper is organized as follows. Section 2 briefly introduces the node failure time and the LWLR algorithm. Section 3 describes the details of the updated network split probability model and the leadership transfer algorithm. Section 4 presents the predicted node failure time and calculates its accuracy. In addition, we tested the cluster's TPS with faulty nodes and the TPS after leadership was transferred. The conclusions and future work are provided in Sect. 5. The research frame is shown in Fig. 1.

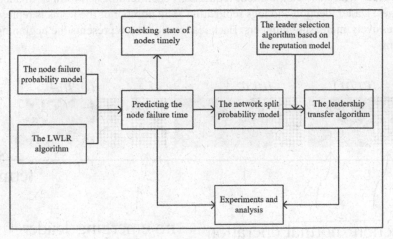

Fig. 1. The research frame.

2 The Node Failure Time and the LWLR Algorithm

2.1 Raft Overview

The Raft algorithm divides all nodes into three states: leader, follower, and candidate. Any node can be in one of three states at any time. Figure 2 shows the node states' transition rule–leader election.

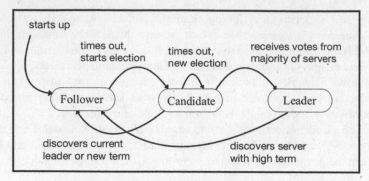

Fig. 2. The node states transition rule of the Raft algorithm [2].

If there is a leader in the cluster, the leader sends periodic heartbeats to all followers to maintain its authority. If a follower does not receive heartbeats during an election timeout, it considers the cluster has not a useful leader. Then the follower transitions to the candidate and invites other nodes to vote for it [2].

The Raft algorithm's term rule is shown in Fig. 3. It divides time into terms, with only a leader who handles the client requests in each term. Each term is divided into two stages: leader election and logs replication. The number of the terms is represented by successively increasing numbers. Each leader election represents the beginning of a new term.

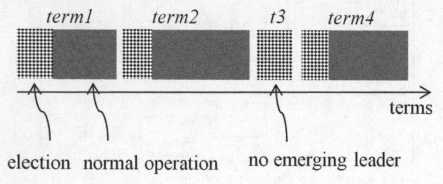

Fig. 3. The term rule of the Raft algorithm [2].

If a candidate obtains the majority of votes, it becomes the leader. If a candidate finds a leader with the same or newer term when waiting for votes, it returns to the follower state.

If many followers become candidates at the same time, the votes are split so that no candidate obtains the majority of votes. Now every candidate times out again, indicating that a new term has begun, just like the t3 in Fig. 3. The Raft algorithm stipulates every follower randomly selects an election timeout from a fixed interval (such as 150 ms–300 ms) to avoid the votes split.

2.2 The Node Failure Time

If the number of faulty nodes exceeds half of the network size, the network is split. There are two main reasons for a follower becoming a faulty node. First, the follower's hardware is faulty. Second, the non-negligible heartbeat loss rate between the leader and the follower decides the node states. Assume that a follower's election timeout is e, and the heartbeat interval is g, then the follower becomes a candidate after losing k $= e/g$ heartbeats consecutively (i.e., the size of election timeout can be expressed as k heartbeats). However, there is still a leader in the cluster, and other nodes ignore the candidate's voting requests. We believe that the candidates have become faulty nodes because they are unable to participate in consensus once more. We made definitions for some words (Table 1).

Table 1. The parameters used to calculate the node failure time.

The parameters	
The network size	N
The number of faulty nodes	f
The heartbeat loss rate	p
Election timeout	$k(e)$
The heartbeat interval	g
The number of heartbeats sent by the leader	n

Definition 1. **The Node Failure:** Given a follower's p and k, the behavior that a follower becomes a faulty node due to consecutively losing k heartbeats is called the node failure. And the time that the follower becomes a faulty node is called the node failure time.

Definition 2. **The Node Failure Probability:** Given a follower's p and k, when the leader sends n-th heartbeat to a follower, the probability that the follower becomes a faulty node is called the node failure probability.

    A heartbeat is the basic unit of the node failure time. So, the node failure time refers to the number of heartbeats sent by the leader when the node failure probability of a follower reaches 1. The longer the node failure time is, the more stable the follower is.

    In addition, the node failure probability is determined directly by election timeout. The longer election timeout, the lower probability of the follower becoming a faulty node is. For example, when $p = 0.05$, if $k = 4$, the node failure probability is 0.05^4 in an election timeout. If $k = 5$, the failure probability is 0.05^5 in an election timeout.

    Given a follower's p and k, the process of the follower becoming a faulty node can be modeled as a binary Markov chain. The node failure probability is obtained from the Markov transition probability matrix, and the longer the node runs, the greater the node failure probability is. For a more detailed node failure probability model, please refer to [12]. We used MATLAB2018 to calculate the node failure time with different p and k.

The result shows the node failure time varies greatly. For example, if $k = 4$, the node failure time is 2.33×10^8 heartbeats when $p = 0.01$, but it is 1.47×10^8 heartbeats when $p = 0.02$. Most importantly, the required program running time to calculate the node failure time are 2902 s and 158 s. It means we must take a lot of time and computing resources to calculate the node failure time. Therefore, we used a machine learning algorithm to predict the node failure time.

2.3 The LWLR Algorithm

We discovered that the relationship between p and the node failure time is similar to the inverse proportional curve in the first quadrant when calculating the node failure time for the input dataset, w When $k = 3$, the curve connected by the training data points is shown in Fig. 4. Therefore, the ordinary linear regression cannot obtain accurate results or even arise under-fitting. The LWLR algorithm avoids under-fitting by giving a certain weight to the test point and nearby points [16], it is very suitable for predicting the node failure time.

In the input dataset, features are p and k, and the labels are the node failure time. Half of the dataset is used for training, and the other half is used for testing. Please refer to Section 4 for more information.

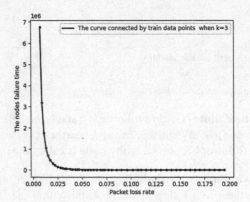

Fig. 4. The curve connected by train data points when $k = 3$.

After importing the input dataset, the LWLR algorithm uses the kernel function to give higher weight to the points close to a test point. And then conducts general linear regression on the corresponding subset (including the test point and the points with weight). The most common kernel function is the Gaussian kernel,

$$W = \exp\left[\frac{\left(x^{(i)} - x\right)^2}{-2\tau^2}\right], \tag{1}$$

where W is a weight matrix containing only diagonal elements, $W = diag\{a_{11}, a_{22}, ..., a_{ii}\}$. Equation (1) indicates that the points closer to the test point have higher weights. τ is a weight parameter, which determines how many the points near the test point are weighted. Higher τ means that more points are used to train the regression model. When $\tau = 1$, all points have the same weight. Different datasets are suitable for different τ, so when training the regression model, it is necessary to repeatedly look for the τ with the smallest error.

As seen in Eq. (2), the LWLR algorithm's objective function is slightly in contrast from general linear regression,

$$J(\theta) = \frac{1}{2} \sum_i W \left[y^{(i)} - \theta^T x^{(i)} \right]^2. \tag{2}$$

To obtain the regression coefficient θ, take the derivative of the objective function and set it to 0,

$$\theta = (X^T W X)^{-1} X^T W y. \tag{3}$$

3 The Leadership Transfer Algorithm

The consensus cannot be complete during the network split, calculating the network split probability and replacing the leader in advance can ensure the cluster's normal operation.

The leader cannot be chosen randomly because it largely determines the cluster performance. We propose a leader selection algorithm based on a reputation model. It can evaluate the follower's stability according to load, delay, the number of lost heartbeats, and the logs index.

3.1 The Network Split Probability Model

The nodes have different heartbeat loss rates p, the existing model is no longer applicable [12]. We used the deformed total probability formula to update the network split probability model. Note that the probability used in the modeling process is the node failure probability calculated based on the heartbeat loss rate. The modeling process is as follows.

① The network size is N, one leader, m normal followers, so there are $N - m - 1$ faulty nodes, and $N - m - 1 \le (N - 1)/2$. Numbering the normal followers from 1 to m makes the modeling more organized, but it's not needed in code. The nodes failure probabilities of m followers are $p_1^n, p_2^n, \ldots\ldots, p_m^n$.

② When the leader sends the $(n + 1)$-th heartbeat, the event that i ($i = 0, 1, 2, \ldots, (m - 1)/2$) followers become faulty nodes is called A_i. The network does not split when A_i occurs, $A_i = A_0 \cup A_1 \cup A_2 \cup \ldots \cup A_{(m-1)/2}$.

③ A_0 means there is no faulty node. A_1 means that only one follower becomes a faulty node. On the premise that A_1 occurs, the event that follower No.1 becomes the faulty node is called A_{11}, and so on, $A_1 = A_{11} \cup A_{12} \cup \ldots\ldots \cup A_{1m}$, so we can obtain the A_1's probability,

$$P(A_1) = \sum_{j=1}^{C_m^1} P(A_{1j}) \tag{4}$$

④ A_2 means that there are two followers become faulty nodes. The followers have different heartbeat loss rate, we must calculate the A_2's probability by permutating and combining the followers. We defined the order of elements and events.

Definition 3. **The order of elements**: mapping the node failure probabilities of the NO.1-NO.m followers set as $1 \times m$ matrix and giving orders to the matrix elements, the matrix is $\left[p_1^n, p_2^n, \ldots \ldots, p_m^n\right]$.

Definition 4. **The order of events**: when there are i ($2 \le i \le (m-1)/2$) followers become faulty nodes, we must decide what i followers are faulty nodes. There are C_m^i combination methods and we called the combining event is $A_{ij}, j \in \left[1, C_m^i\right]$. Starting with the first element p_1^n, there is an order between the events obtained by traversing and combining elements from front to back.

For example, in A_2, the event in which followers NO.1 and NO.2 become faulty nodes is A_{21}, the event in which followers NO.1 and NO.3 become faulty nodes is A_{22}, and so on, the event in which followers NO.$(m-1)$ and NO.m become faulty nodes is $A_{2C_m^2}$, then the A_2's probability is

$$P(A_2) = \sum_{j=1}^{C_m^2} P(A_{2j}).$$ (5)

⑤ The $A_{(m-1)/2}$'s probability is

$$P\left(A_{\frac{m-1}{2}}\right) = \sum_{j=1}^{C_m^{\frac{m-1}{2}}} P\left(A_{\frac{m-1}{2}j}\right).$$ (6)

⑥ The probability P_N that the network does not split can be obtained by adding the probability of A_i,

$$P_N = \sum_{j=1}^{C_m^i} \sum_{i=1}^{\frac{m-1}{2}} P(A_{ij}).$$ (7)

⑦ Therefore, the network split probability P_Y when the leader sends the $(n+1)$-th heartbeat is

$$P_Y = 1 - P_N = 1 - \sum_{j=1}^{C_m^i} \sum_{i=1}^{\frac{m-1}{2}} P\left(A_{ij}\right).$$ (8)

We can calculate the network split probability of any time, prevent the network split by transferring leadership when the network split probability is too high.

3.2   The Leader Selection Algorithm

The Reputation Model

The data only flows from the leader to the followers, the TPS of the Raft algorithm is closely related to the leader. A highly stable leader can improve consensus efficiency and reduce the network split probability. Therefore, evaluating the node's stability is critical when selecting the next leader. The node's stability depends on many factors, such as load, delay, the logs index, and the number of lost heartbeats.

The load refers to the network load rate of the followers, it is expressed as a percentage usually. The delay refers to one-way communication time between the leader and the followers, and the normal delay is between 20 ms–100 ms approximately. The number of lost heartbeats is re-accumulated from 0 at the beginning of a new term. So, if a follower has a smaller load, delay, or the number of lost heartbeats, it is more stable. Suppose the follower's log and the current leader's log differ only on the last log index, a follower is more stable if it has a bigger last log index.

Assume that a follower's load is L, the delay is T, and the number of lost heartbeats is H. The ratio of logs index is $M = M_f/M_p$, M_f is the last log index of the follower, M_p is the last log index of the leader, and $M \leq 1$ according to the Leader Completeness [2].

The reputation value of the follower as follows,

$$Value = \frac{\alpha}{L} + \frac{\beta}{T} + \frac{\gamma}{H} + \frac{1}{\epsilon}\exp(M). \tag{9}$$

α, β, γ, and ε are the proportional coefficients, which represent the importance of each factor. The reputation value decreases when L, T, and H increase, or M decreases. Because the reputation values are calculated by the followers, they cannot be normalized. According to the numerical characteristics of L, T, H, and M, we set $\alpha + \beta + \gamma + \varepsilon = 100$, $\alpha = \beta = 40$, and $\gamma = \varepsilon = 10$. The proportional coefficients can be flexibly adjusted to suit various application scenarios. For example, increasing α and γ in the certification system requires a leader to have higher stability, or increasing β in the transaction system requires a leader to have a lower delay.

The reputation model digitally represents the follower's stability and provides the basis for selecting a stable leader, thereby improving the consensus efficiency and stability of the Raft algorithm.

The Leader Selection Algorithm

A follower with a higher reputation value is more stable and better suited as a leader. However, if the follower with the highest reputation value is always selected as the next leader, it lacks randomness. We designed a leader selection algorithm. When the current leader selects the next leader, first it selects the top 20% of followers as the '*candidate*' for the next leader according to their reputation values, then generates a random number for each '*candidate*' [18]. Assume that the reputation value of a '*candidate*' is $Value_i$, and its random number is z_i, the weight of the '*candidate*' for becoming the next leader is

$$W_i = z_i \times Value_i. \tag{10}$$

The current leader appoints the '*candidate*' with the highest weight as the next leader,

$$Leader = \max(W_i). \tag{11}$$

3.3 The Leadership Transfer Algorithm

Faulty nodes cannot participate in consensus, and the current leader sends AppendEntries RPCs to faulty nodes indefinitely [2] so that the consensus efficiency of the Raft algorithm is affected. The leadership transfer algorithm replaces the leader and adds a mechanism to make faulty nodes back to work. It includes the following steps.

1. When the network split probability reaches 80% or the number of faulty nodes $f = (N - 1)/2$, the current leader sends a reputation request to all followers. This request includes the current leader's ID, address, term, last log index, and timestamp.
2. The followers who received the request calculate their reputation value and return it to the current leader, along with their ID and address.
3. The current leader selects the next leader by the leader selection algorithm. And then the current leader updates the logs of the next leader using the normal log replication.
4. The current leader stops processing client requests when it and the next leader have the same logs. And then it sends a leadership transfer message to all followers. This message contains the next leader's ID and address, as well as the leadership transfer flag. The current leader increments its term and returns to the follower state.
5. If a follower and the next leader have the same ID and address, the follower directly becomes the leader, increments its term, and sends heartbeats to other nodes. If their ID and address differ from the next leader's, the follower sets the next leader as the current leader according to the ID and address from the leadership transfer message, increments its term, and remains the follower state.
6. The term of faulty nodes is greater than the new leader, they cannot return to follower state after receiving heartbeats from the new leader. We designed a mechanism for faulty nodes. They first clean their data after receiving the leadership transfer flag, later restart and rejoin the cluster as new followers, and the current leader updates their logs by the consistency check.
7. The leadership is transferred, and the cluster conducts logs replication normally.

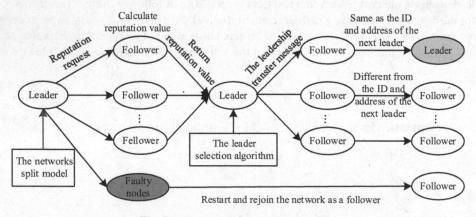

Fig. 5. The leadership transfer algorithm.

Figure 5 briefly describes the leadership transfer algorithm. After the next leader receives the leadership transfer message, it no longer waits for election timeout, but directly becomes the leader. It avoids the votes split, keeps from the network split, and makes faulty nodes get out of candidate state to participate in the consensus again. In Sect. 4 we evaluate whether it can improve Raft's consensus efficiency.

4 Simulation and Analysis

4.1 Experimental Environment

The experiment was divided into two parts. The experiment that predicted node failure time using the LWLR algorithm was performed on a Core i7 8-core 3.00 GHz computer with 48 GB memory, and the development environment is Python 3.8. The leadership transfer algorithm was conducted by simulating a multi-node environment by configuring multiple virtual machines in LinuxMint19.3/Golang1.14.3.

4.2 Using the LWLR Algorithm to Predict the Node Failure Time

Predicting the Node Failure Time
According to p and k, we used MATLAB2018 to calculate the node failure time, and then obtain the input dataset of the LWLR algorithm. The dataset's contents are shown in Table 2, it contains 420 pieces of data. To better avoid the followers becoming faulty nodes, the node failure time was set to the time when the node failure probability reaches 0.9.

Assuming that the heartbeats interval is 100ms, we set the range of election timeout as 300 ms–699 ms, i.e., $k = 3, 4, 5$, and 6. When the heartbeat loss rate $p = 0.2$, even if $k = 6$, the follower becomes a faulty node after about 46000 heartbeats (1.3 h), so we set the range of heartbeat loss rate at 0–0.2.

Table 2. The contents of the dataset.

The heartbeat loss rate	Election timeout	The node failure time
p_1	k_1	t_1
$\vdots$	$\vdots$	$\vdots$
p_{420}	k_{420}	t_{420}

To make prediction easier, we divided the data into four groups according to election timeout to conduct a lot of training. Figure 6(a)–(d) shows the predicted node failure time (i.e., the regression curve) after logarithmic transformation. The dots are the train data points, and the intersections are the test data points. The majority of the data points are located on or around the regression curve, and then we performed the error analysis to evaluate the accuracy of the predicted results.

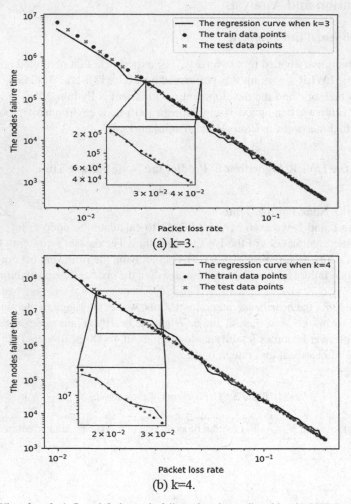

(a) k=3.

(b) k=4.

Fig. 6. When $k = 3, 4, 5,$ and 6, the node failure time is predicted by the LWLR algorithm.

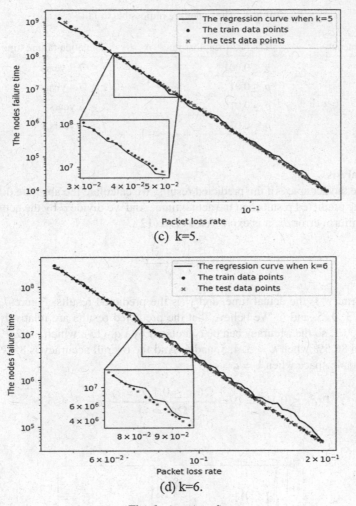

(c) k=5.

(d) k=6.

Fig. 6. (*continued*)

The abscissa axes of Fig. 6(a)–(d) are not the same. When p is very small, the node failure time is too long. We believe that some nodes are unlikely to fail. As seen in Table 3. When $k = 3$ and $p = 0.001$, the follower becomes a faulty node after about 2.3×10^9 heartbeats, which is about 7.3 years.

Table 3. The nodes are impossible to fail.

Election timeout	The heartbeat loss rate	The node failure time
$k = 3$	$p \leq 0.001$	$t \geq 7.3$ years
$k = 4$	$p \leq 0.01$	$t \geq 7.4$ years
$k = 5$	$p \leq 0.016$	$t \geq 7$ years
$k = 6$	$p \leq 0.032$	$t \geq 7$ years

Error Analysis

To evaluate the accuracy of the predicted results, we calculate the absolute difference d between the predicted results and the actual time. And we divide d by the actual time to obtain a uniform error dr, it is expressed as Eq. (12),

$$dr = \frac{|y^i - \tilde{y}^i|}{y^i}. \tag{12}$$

Among them, y^i is the actual time, and $\tilde{y}^i$ is the predicted results. Figure 7 shows dr when $k = 3, 4, 5$, and 6. We believe that the predicted results are relatively accurate when $dr \leq 0.1$, so the accuracy can be calculated by Eq. (13), which is 82.7%, 92.3%, 81.5%, and 86.5% when $k = 3, 4, 5$, and 6. And the overall accuracy is 85.7%. $\Omega(k = i)$ is the sample space when $k = i$,

$$P(dr \leq 0.1 | k = i) = \frac{\Omega(dr \leq 0.1, k = i)}{\Omega(k = i)}, i = 3, 4, 5, 6. \tag{13}$$

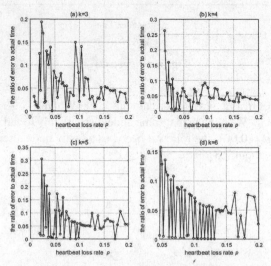

Fig. 7. The ratio of d to the actual time.

The sum of mean square errors r be utilized to analyze the influence of τ on the predicted results,

$$r = \sum_i \left(y^i - \tilde{y}^i \right)^2. \tag{14}$$

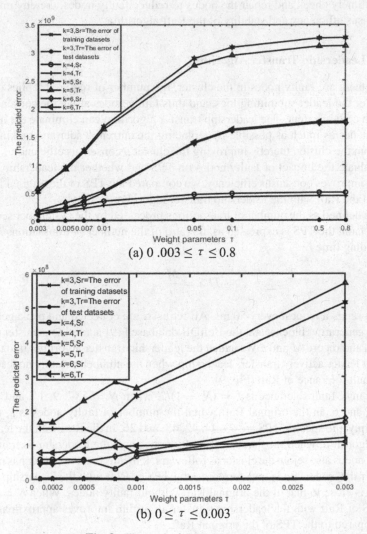

(a) $0.003 \le \tau \le 0.8$

(b) $0 \le \tau \le 0.003$

Fig. 8. The sum of mean square error r.

We draw Fig. 8(a)–(b) for ease of observation. They present the training dataset error S_r and test dataset error T_r at different weight parameters τ. When $\tau \ge 0.001$, S_r and T_r will increase with τ, it is because the difference in the node failure time is too large. If we consider too many data points, there will be greater errors. When $0.00008 \le \tau \le$

0.001, there is no specific rule. This is not surprising, different datasets are suitable for different τ. In addition, S_r and T_r of all datasets are the same when $\tau = 0.00008$ and $\tau = 0.0002$. We must select the appropriate τ to obtain the best predicted time. Therefore, when $k = 3, 5$, and 6, $\tau = 0.0002$, when $k = 4, \tau = 0.001$.

The LWLR algorithm was utilized to predict the node states by predicting the node failure time, which provides input data for the network split probability model, or relevant staffs can timely check and repair the nodes to reduce faulty nodes, thereby improving the consensus efficiency and stability of the Raft algorithm.

4.3 The Leadership Transfer Algorithm

Although there are faulty nodes in the cluster, the number of required replies does not decrease for the leader submitting logs, and thus faulty nodes affect the consensus efficiency to a certain extent. The leadership transfer algorithm can eliminate the influence of faulty nodes as much as possible by replacing the current leader and making faulty nodes rejoin the cluster, thereby improving the cluster's consensus efficiency.

To evaluate the impact of faulty nodes on TPS and whether the leadership transfer algorithm improves consensus efficiency, we compared the TPS of the original Raft and the TPS of the Raft with the leadership transfer algorithm.

TPS is defined as the number of transactions processed by the system per second. In the blockchain, the TPS is expressed as the ratio of the number of transactions M to the corresponding time t,

$$TPS = \frac{M}{t}. \tag{15}$$

The client sends a request every 50 ms. All requests are collected and packaged by the leader for generating blocks, and the BoltDB database [19] is used to persistently store block data and record M and t. We added the leadership transfer algorithm into the Raft, the current leader actively transfers leadership when the number of faulty nodes reaches the max fault tolerance of Raft (Fig. 9).

Raft's max fault tolerance is $f = (N - 1)/2$, when $N = 5, 7, 9, 11$, and 13, $f = 2, 3, 4, 5$, and 6. In the original Raft, when the number of faulty nodes is f, the TPS drops sharply, the specific TPS are 43, 44, 42, 43, and 26. In the Raft with the leadership transfer algorithm, when the number of faulty nodes is f, the leadership is transferred, and faulty nodes also rejoin the cluster as followers. It means that the cluster has no faulty nodes after the leadership is transferred, so the TPS of Raft with the leadership transfer algorithm is close to that of the original Raft without faulty nodes. When $N = 13, f = 6$, the TPS of Raft with the leadership transfer algorithm improves approximately 500 times compared to the TPS of the original Raft.

In addition, the leadership transfer algorithm sets that the next leader does not need to wait for election timeout and start a new leader election, thus avoiding vote split. This is good news for clusters with too many faulty nodes, because the more faulty nodes, the more elections are required to elect the next leader [6, 12].

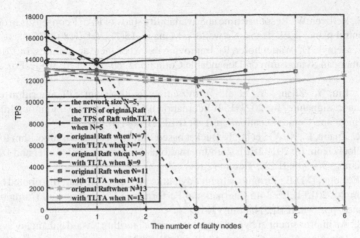

Fig. 9. The TPS of Raft with the leadership transfer algorithm (TLTA) and the original Raft.

5 Conclusion

Faulty nodes affect the consensus efficiency, and the network split causes the Raft cluster cannot complete consensus for client requests. Therefore, we reduced the number of faulty nodes and kept from the network split by the LWLR algorithm and the leadership transferring algorithm. The node states predicted by the LWLR algorithm be used to predict the network split probability, or relevant staffs can timely check the node states to ensure that they are in the follower state. Later, we updated the network split probability model when the node's heartbeat loss rate is different and proposed the leadership transfer algorithm to keep from the network split. The experimental results show that the accuracy of the LWLR algorithm predicting the node failure time is approximately 85.7%, and the leadership transfer can also increase the Raft cluster's TPS considerably.

In the consensus process, the nodes generate a large amount of data that reflect the node's actual situation, such as the delay, the load, and the heartbeat loss rate. In future work, we will combine machine learning and consensus data to improve the performance of the consortium blockchain.

References

1. NAKAMOTO S.: Bitcoin: a peer-to-peer electronic cash system. Decentralized Business Review, 21260 (2008)
2. Ongaro, D.: Consensus: bridging theory and practice. M.S. dissertation, Stanford University, Palo Alto, USA (2014)
3. Hanmer, R., Jagadeesan, L., Mendiratta, V., et al.: Friend or foe: strong consistency vs overload in high-availability distributed systems and SDN. In: 2018 IEEE International Symposium on Software Reliability Engineering Workshops, pp. 59–64. IEEE, Memphis (2018)
4. Dexter, P., Sendir, B., Chiu, K.: Detecting and reacting to anomalies in relaxed uses of Raft. In: 2020 20th IEEE/ACM International Symposium on Cluster, Cloud and Internet Computing, pp. 659–668. IEEE, Melbourne (2020)

5. Sakic, E., Kellerer, W.: Response time and availability study of RAFT consensus in distributed SDN control plane. IEEE Trans. Netw. Serv. Manage. **15**(1), 304–318 (2017)
6. Fluri, C., Melnyk, D., Wattenhofer, R.: Improving raft when there are failures. In: 2018 Eighth Latin-American Symposium on Dependable Computing, pp. 167–170. IEEE, Foz do Iguacu (2018)
7. Tian, S., Liu, Y., Zhang, Y., et al.: A byzantine fault-tolerant raft algorithm combined with Schnorr signature. In: 2021 15th International Conference on Ubiquitous Information Management and Communication, pp. 1–5. IEEE, Seoul (2021)
8. Wang, R., Zhang, L., Xu, Q., et al.: K-Bucket based Raft-like consensus algorithm for permissioned blockchain. In: 2019 IEEE 25th International Conference on Parallel and Distributed Systems, pp. 996–999. IEEE, Tianjin (2019)
9. Pâris, J.F., Long, D.D.E.: Pirogue, a lighter dynamic version of the Raft distributed consensus algorithm. In: 2015 IEEE 34th International Performance Computing and Communications Conference, pp. 1–8. IEEE, Nanjing (2015)
10. Min, B.J.: An improvement of hyperledger fabric raft algorithm toward enhancing availability. J. Korean Inst. Next Gener. Comput. **17**(2), 80–91 (2021)
11. Huang, D., Li, L., Chen, B., et al.: RBFT: byzantine fault-tolerant consensus mechanism based on raft cluster. J. Commun. **42**(3), 209–219 (2021)
12. Gao, S., Yu, T., Zhu, J., Cai, W.: T-PBFT: an EigenTrust-based practical Byzantine fault tolerance consensus algorithm. China Commun. **16**(12), 111–123 (2019)
13. Huang, D., Ma, X., Zhang, S.: Performance analysis of the raft consensus algorithm for private blockchains. IEEE Trans. Syst. Man Cybern.: Syst. **50**(1), 172–181 (2019)
14. Xu, H., Zhang, L., Liu, Y., et al.: Raft based wireless blockchain networks in the presence of malicious jamming. IEEE Wirel. Commun. Lett. **9**(6), 817–821 (2020)
15. Wang, K., Li, Y., Ma, J., Yan, Z., Guo, S., Yan, Y.: Design and implementation of a charging station transaction system based on blockchain. In: Liu, Q., Liu, X., Chen, B., Zhang, Y., Peng, J. (eds.) Proceedings of the 11th International Conference on Computer Engineering and Networks. LNEE, vol. 808, pp. 1315–1325. Springer, Singapore (2022). https://doi.org/10.1007/978-981-16-6554-7_147
16. Han, B., Zhang, Y., Ou, Q., et al.: A double incentive trading mechanism for IoT and blockchain based electricity trading in local energy market. In: In: Liu, Q., Liu, X., Chen, B., Zhang, Y., Peng, J. (eds.) Proceedings of the 11th International Conference on Computer Engineering and Networks. LNEE, vol. 808, pp. 3–12. Springer, Singapore (2022). https://doi.org/10.1007/978-981-16-6554-7_1
17. Harrington, P.: Machine Learning in Action. Simon and Schuster, USA (2012)
18. Gu, R., Chen, B., Huang, D.: Primary node selection algorithm of PBFT based on anomaly detection and reputation model. In: Liu, Q., Liu, X., Chen, B., Zhang, Y., Peng, J. (eds.) Proceedings of the 11th International Conference on Computer Engineering and Networks. LNEE, vol. 808, pp. 1613–1622. Springer, Singapore (2022). https://doi.org/10.1007/978-981-16-6554-7_178
19. Ben, J.: BoltDB: an embedded key/value database for Go. https://github.com/boltdb/bolt. Accessed 19 Aug 2020

Blockchain Multi-signature Wallet System Based on QR Code Communication

Hongxin Zhang[1], Xin Zou[1], Guanghuan Xie[1], and Zhuo Li[2(✉)]

[1] College of Computer Science and Technology, Zhejiang University,
Hangzhou 310058, China
{zhx,22160282,looper}@zju.edu.cn
[2] Global Technology Service, State Street Technology (Zhejiang) Ltd.,
Hangzhou 310013, China
lizhuo@zju.edu.cn

Abstract. In order to avoid the risk of theft and loss of the private key of the blockchain wallet, a novel secure and stable blockchain multi-party signature system combining software and hardware is proposed. First, at the software level, multi-party key management method is adopted to divide the blockchain wallet key into multiple fragments for multi-point storage. Threshold signature technology is adopted to provide key escrow and retrieval services. Then a cold wallet for storing keys is designed at the hardware level. In order to avoid the risk of being attacked by hackers through network contact, a visible light communication method based on Quick Response Code is proposed. The Base45 coding scheme is adopted to improve the coding efficiency of QR Code, and the GG18 multi-party signature process is optimized. Finally, this paper analyzes the security of visible light communication, and verifies the efficiency of this method by experiments.

Keywords: Blockchain · Secure multi-party computing · Hardware wallet · QR Code encoding · Visible light communication · Digital asset escrow

1 Introduction

In blockchain transactions, users need to use the key for transaction signature, which is independent of the real identity. Therefore, the key controls the whole life system of the wallet, and the leakage of the key will cause irreparable loss to the assets stored in the wallet address. Key management includes storage, backup, recovery, and transaction review, and it requires high security and standardization. For common users, there is a need to digital asset escrow service.

Digital asset escrow services refer to digital currency escrow and trading services provided by third parties. There are various forms of escrow, such as wallets, custodians, etc. The core service is to provide digital currency deposits and withdrawals. Since the development of digital asset custodians, the leading well-known institutions such as BitGO, Coinbase, ItBit and Xapo have accumulated a lot of advantages in terms of customers, funds and brands. Due to the high barriers to trust and sales in the digital asset escrow industry, the industry is not friendly to startups. To gain the trust of users, the compliance and security of the hosting system have become the primary optimization indicators. This paper builds a digital asset escrow system, which realizes private key multi-party escrow and transaction multi-party signature based on homomorphic encryption and threshold signature technology, and provides private key retrieval services; A hardware wallet for storing private keys is designed. The communication method based on QR Code scanning ensures that the private key is completely stored offline and disconnected from the network. A defense scheme is proposed for potential electromagnetic side-channel attacks. Finally, the Base45-based QR Code encoding method is used to optimize the encoding and communication efficiency. With the design of software and hardware coordination, a reliable and safe digital asset escrow scheme is proposed.

2   Related Works

Digital wallet keys are crucial for digital asset owners, and owners must consider how to manage wallet keys securely. At present, the mainstream key management methods are as follows: 1) Local key storage: these keys can be accessed through the designated location of the local device. The advantage is that it is convenient, but it is vulnerable to attack. 2) Encrypted wallet [15]: the user protects the key by setting a password, and only by entering the correct password can he have access to the key. For instance, Schindler [24] proposed a cryptocurrency wallet management system based on a semi-trust social network. However, this key storage method is vulnerable to brute force attacks. 3) Offline storage [23]: the key is stored on an offline USB device or recorded on a paper file, which sacrifices the convenience of key access. 4) Key escrow: the key is managed by a digital asset escrow organization. Wang [25] proposed a session key escrow scheme based on threshold cryptography and proved the security of the proposed key escrow scheme under the assumption of elliptic curve discrete logarithm (ECDL).

The International Organization for Standardization (ISO)/Technical Committee (TC) 307 ISO 22739:2020 Blockchain and Distributed Ledger Technology-Glossary defines a wallet as "an application used to generate, manage, store assets or applications that use private and public keys", which "may be implemented as a software or hardware module". It has been realized to store the key on the hardware wallet which is disconnected from the network. At present, several popular hardware wallets in the market, such as Ledger Nano X, Trezor One, Keep Key and Ledger Nano S, all have their own service functions and mature security guarantee methods. Their common features are small and portable, completely disconnected from the Internet, and connected to computer devices through USB or Bluetooth, as shown in Fig. 1.

These hardware wallets are designed to be secure without sacrificing convenience, but the need to use USB or Bluetooth connections to communicate with

Fig. 1. Common hardware wallets. From left to right are Ledger Nano X, Trezor One, Keep Key, Ledger Nano S

computer devices still leaves a possible avenue for hackers to attack. Nikolay Ivanov [16] proposed an attack method using clipboard, designed and implemented a malware named EthClipper, and tested the attack against the above popular hardware wallets. The test showed that the attacker had a 50% probability to complete the attack. The makers of these wallets have also confirmed the dangers of the attack. On January 26, 2022, a hardware hacker exploited a vulnerability related to RAM reading to break into a Trezor One hardware wallet containing over $2 million, and Trezor officials urgently fixed the vulnerability. However, hardware wallet is still the most secure choice for digital currency users to store their keys. How to ensure the security is the way forward of hardware wallet design.

3   System Overview

The disadvantage of single point storage of keys is that the loss of keys can result in the loss of all tokens if no backup is prepared. In order to solve the above shortcomings, multi-party signature protocols based on secure multi-party computation are proposed, and multi-party signature systems develop rapidly [4,6,7,10,12,19]. In this paper, a digital asset escrow system is constructed. Users entrust part of their keys to the escrow system for management. The escrow system also provides key recovery service, and helps users review transaction details and manage digital assets.

3.1   Distributed Key Management

The escrow system includes an on-chain software hot wallet part and a hardware cold wallet part for storing private keys. The hot wallet system adopts a multi-party signature scheme to ensure that the appearance of a single malicious party will not seriously affect the transaction. The key is generated by the central system machine, and then divided into three parts, which are respectively handed over to the three parties for storage. The threshold signature scheme is adopted, and single party cannot perform opaque operations on the account. At the same time, transaction processing does not require the participation of all three parties, which ensures the convenience of multi-party signatures. There are three types of roles in the multi-signature software system, each of which is assigned different permissions and functions by the software system: 1) Investment manager: have the right to view the user's assets and transaction information, send currency trading requests as the client's agent, and have the right to send key reset requests when the key is lost. 2) Operator: handles requests sent by users in a timely manner, is responsible for communicating with digital currency exchanges, responding to currency trading requests, and has the right to initiate key recovery requests. 3) Administrator: manages a part of the keys of all users of the escrow company, and does not participate in the processing of ordinary transactions. The managed keys are used in key recovery scenarios.

3.2   Private Key Share Cold Storage

In order to ensure the convenience of the signature process, the common private key share stored in the cloud is used to complete multi-party signature for ordinary transactions with a small amount of money. For important transactions with large amounts and serious consequences for property loss, the escrow system will require the use of private key shares stored in the cold wallet to sign.

The cold wallet system is used to store important private key shares and completely disconnected form the network. The private key shares are stored on the physical device and are powered off when not in use. The physical device is small in size, portable and has computing processing capabilities. It can be started quickly when important transaction signatures are required. It accepts external messages through visible light communication and calculates and responds to messages. GG18 (Proposed by Rosario Gennaro and Steven Goldfeder in 2018 [10]) scheme is adopted in the signature process [17]. While ensuring security through multiple rounds of interaction, physically-assisted signature design is adopted to improve the convenience of use.

3.3   Multi-party Signature Process

For large-volume and small-value transactions, in order to improve transaction efficiency, only the investment manager and the operator need to provide the key for signing, and the administrator does not participate in the transaction signing, as shown in Fig. 2.

When the user's key shares are lost and the user initiates a key recovery request, the operator will receive a request message and contact the user for offline confirmation. After confirming that the key is lost, the unfinished transaction order will be frozen first, and then the administrator who has key share will be notified, and the key will be regenerated using the 2/3 threshold signature principle. The new key will be divided into three parts by the system machine and assigned to three roles, the process is shown in Fig. 3.

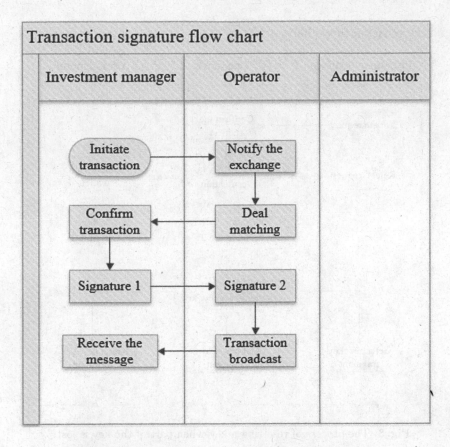

Fig. 2. The process of conducting ordinary transactions.

4 Multi-party Signature Implementation

4.1 Practicability of Multi-signature Scheme

The DSA/ECDSA algorithm for signatures has gained much attention in recent years due to the popularity of Bitcoin and other digital currencies. There has been a lot of research on this, Gennaro et al. [13,14] proposed a threshold scheme for DSA, but this scheme has not been well applied because it requires $2t+1$ participants for signature. In [19], the first truly practical full threshold ECDSA signing protocol that has both fast signing and fast key distribution was presented. In the same year, Gennaro [10] proposed a new threshold optimal protocol to support efficient distributed key generation. We find that GG18 signature scheme can perform faster signature, reduce the amount of transmitted data and running time, and meet the application requirements of most existing wallet management scenarios. Therefore, the wallet system proposed in this paper is built based on GG18 signature scheme.

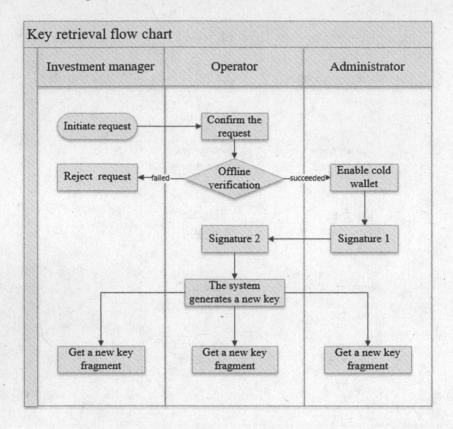

Fig. 3. The process of resetting a key when part of the key is lost.

4.2   Signature Algorithm

An encrypted currency signature algorithm system S based on asymmetric encryption needs to include the following three basic parts:

1) Key generation function $KeyGen$:

$$(sk, pk) = KeyGen(1^\lambda) \tag{1}$$

The input parameter 1^λ is the system security parameter, and the one-to-one corresponding private key sk and public key pk are returned;

2) Signature function Sig:

$$\sigma = Sig(sk, m) \tag{2}$$

It is used to sign the message m with some randomness in the case of known private key sk.

3) Verification function Ver:

$$b = Ver(pk, m, \sigma) \tag{3}$$

To do verification with the corresponding public key pk and return a boolean value.

The signature algorithms adopted by mainstream blockchains such as Bitcoin and Ethereum are all based on ECDSA [2,3,9,21]. Without loss of generality, this paper only discusses cryptocurrencies based on ECDSA [18], which is based on the multiplication on elliptic curves. There exists a cyclic group G on an elliptic curve whose order is prime q. Define multiplication within a cyclic group:

$$P = x \times G \tag{4}$$

where G is the generator of cyclic group G, x belongs to Zq, P is the result of calculation which is the point on the elliptic curve. It is difficult to compute x when only the generator G and the product P are known. On this basis, define:

1) Key generation: select the number X_k randomly in the group Zq and calculate:

$$P_k = X_k \times G \tag{5}$$

where X_k is the private key and P_k is the public key.

2) Signature: for message m to be signed, hash functions $H(m)$, $k \in Z_q$ are defined to generate temporary key pair, where:

$$R = k \times G \tag{6}$$

Then take r as the abscissa of R and calculate:

$$s = k^{-1}(H(m) + x_k \times r) \bmod q \tag{7}$$

and output the signature:

$$\sigma = (r, s) \tag{8}$$

3) Signature verification: check if $r \in Z_q$ and $s \in Z_q$, then calculate:

$$R^{'} = s^{-1}(H(m) \times G + r \times P_k) \tag{9}$$

Take the abscissa of $R^{'}$, which is named as $r^{'}$, and output True if $r^{'} = r$, False otherwise.

4.3   Homomorphic Encryption

At present, multi-signature protocols mostly rely on homomorphic encryption [1]. In homomorphic encryption, the result of a ciphertext operation remains ciphertext. For example, $Enc(\cdot)$ is defined as the encryption algorithm of additive homomorphism encryption. For the ciphertext $c_1 = Enc(a)$, $c_2 = Enc(b)$, there exists the operation $\oplus$ such that:

$$c_1 \oplus c_2 = Enc(a + b) \tag{10}$$

The additive homomorphism also implies scalar multiplication operation. For ciphertext $c = Enc(m)$, plaintext a, there exists operation $\otimes$, which makes:

$$a \otimes c = Enc(am) \tag{11}$$

4.4   Secret Sharing

In threshold signature scheme, the implementation depends largely on secret sharing protocol. In the secret sharing protocol, a secret value can be shared in the form of (t, n) threshold, that is, the secret value can be shared with n parties, and the secret value can be restored only when at least t parties participate. In secret sharing, if the dealer wants to share the secret value s in the form of (t, n) threshold, the $t - 1$ polynomial will be generated randomly:

$$f(x) = s + \sum_{i=1}^{t-1} a_i x^i \tag{12}$$

The fixed constant term is the secret value to be shared. The secret holder calculates $f(1), f(2)...f(n)$ and send them to the corresponding n players. For a degree $t - 1$ polynomial, if t points on it are already known, the polynomial can be restored. Therefore, any t-parties can restore the entire polynomial to compute the secret value s.

Secret sharing shards also support addition operations. For example, when the secret sharer shares two secret values a, b to n participants in the form of (t, n) threshold, two $t - 1$ polynomials A, B are generated:

$$f_a(x) = a + \sum_{i=1}^{t-1} a_i x^i \tag{13}$$

$$f_b(x) = b + \sum_{i=1}^{t-1} b_i x^i \tag{14}$$

When the participants need to calculate the target value $c = a + b$, there is a polynomial C such that:

$$f_c(x) = c + \sum_{i=1}^{t-1} C_i x^i = f_a(x) + f_b(x) \tag{15}$$

For any participant P_j, knowing the fragments $f_a(j)$ and $f_b(j)$ can get the fragment of the polynomial C, so any t participants can calculate the target value $a + b$.

4.5   Threshold Signature

Threshold signature [10] refers to that party N holds the key share, in which any T can generate the corresponding signature. Threshold signature requires that $t - 1$ malicious participants cannot forge the signature of any message. In threshold signature scheme, the signature verification algorithm is usually the same as the single-party signature scheme. Threshold signature protocol consists of two parts: distributed key generation and distributed signing. The distributed key generation process generates key shares for each participant and generates the corresponding public key of the account through interaction. The process of distributed signature is the process of generating signatures for a threshold number of participants. Specifically, for n participants of threshold signature P_1, P_2, P_n, defines the distributed key generation protocol DKG, where any participant P_i has:

$$DKG(1^\lambda) \to (sk_i, pk) \qquad (16)$$

where 1^λ is the security parameter, pk is the generated public key, and sk_i is the fragment of the private key sk. For any t parties involved in distributed key generation such as P_1, P_2, P_t, define distributed signature protocol DS:

$$DS(m, sk_1, sk_2 \ldots sk_k) \to \sigma \qquad (17)$$

where m is the message to be signed and is the generated signature. A valid signature is required to return a boolean value of True for the signature verification algorithm Ver.

5 Communication Mechanism of Cold Wallet

5.1 Cold Wallet Design Concept

Due to the anonymity of blockchain, wallet keys control all the assets of users, so ensuring the security of wallet keys is the goal of all escrow systems. Under this premise, the design concept of the cold wallet is as follows: Firstly, as long as it is a device that contacts the network, there is a risk of being attacked, and the more processes that rely on the network to interact, the easier it is to be attacked. Secondly, there is also the risk of being attacked when using a USB flash drive for data interaction, the USB flash drive injected with a virus may automatically record data. Once it contacts the network again, it is possible to steal the data through the network. For personal stored keys, the advantage of hot storage is that it is convenient, but the disadvantage is that it is easy to be lost or stolen, so it needs to be backed up in different places to ensure security.

5.2 Implementation of Cold Wallet Communication

When the key is stored on a physical device that is completely isolated from the network, its security can be effectively guaranteed. However, during the use of the cold wallet key, it may communicate with the network device. Whether the communication method is safe or not affects the security of the entire cold wallet. Common communication protocols range from wireless channels (such as wifi, bluetooth, NFC [20]) to physical media (such as USB connections). Visible light communication is a communication method that uses light in the visible light band as an information carrier to directly transmit optical signals in the air, and has the security features of anti-interference and anti-interception.

In this paper, the cold wallet of the system is implemented by visible light communication based on QR Code scanning. 1) Camera input: The device that needs to communicate with the cold wallet adopts the encoding method based on Base45 to convert the information into a QR Code and display it to the cold wallet. The cold wallet scans the QR Code displayed by the device with its own camera, obtains the information, stores it, and performs the next calculation. 2) Screen output: After the calculation is completed, the cold wallet needs to transmit a new round of interactive information to the other party's device. Currently, the cold wallet converts the information into a QR Code and displays it on the screen of the cold wallet. After the other party's device scans the code, the information transmitted by the cold wallet can be obtained.

6   Hardware Design of Cold Wallet

The hardware wallet of the system in this paper is mainly composed of an embedded microcomputer for computing and a camera for receiving external interactive information. The microcomputer is a Raspberry Pi 4B, the CPU model is Broadcom BCM2711, the main frequency is 1.5 GHz, and it has 4 cores, ARM Cortex-A72 architecture, and the main board is powered by a 5V USB-C port input. The built-in camera uses a 5-megapixel camera with a size of 32 × 32 (mm), an operating voltage of USB-5V, an interface of USB2.0, a signal-to-noise ratio of 32 dB, a 90° viewing angle, and a focal length of 3.6 mm. The screen used to display the QR Code is a 4 in. DPI LCD. It has 720 × 720 pixels, capacitive touch, and connected to the Raspberry Pi 4B through the 40PIN GPIO interface. The appearance adopts an integrated design to ensure that the inside of the cold wallet cannot be touched. The shell design is shown in Fig. 4.

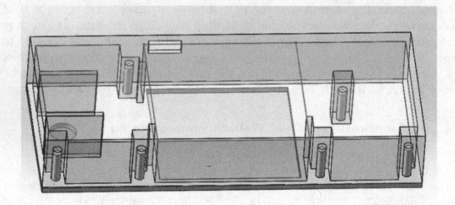

Fig. 4. Shell design of hardware wallet. Three exposed ports for power, display and camera.

The wallet shell only exposes the power interface and camera for power supply and interaction. The middle part is an 84 × 84 (mm) display screen, which is used to display the QR Code: the stability of the information interaction process is realized by physical auxiliary interactive equipment. The device that needs to interact is connected to a display screen and a camera to realize the complete automation of the code scanning process, ensuring security and improving the stability of the code scanning process. The interaction process is shown in Fig. 5.

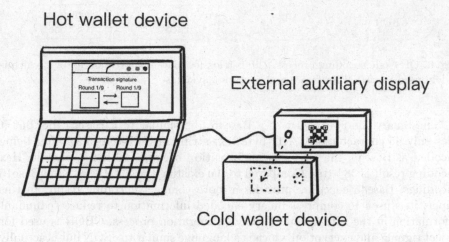

Fig. 5. Schematic diagram of signing interaction with cold wallet.

7 Hardware Design of Cold Wallet

7.1 Common Attacks on Hardware Wallets

At present, most wallets on the market use the communication methods of USB and Bluetooth to cooperate to generate signatures. However, these communication methods do not achieve complete isolation of the network, security needs to be improved. Hardware wallets with these designs can still be attacked in a number of ways. For USB-based devices, there are four main attack methods [22]: 1) Reprogramming the built-in microcontroller of the USB device. 2) Performing malicious operations by reprogramming the firmware of the USB device. 3) Exploiting vulnerabilities when the operating system interacts with the USB protocol. 4) Power attack method.

Bluetooth is a type of wireless network, and the method to attack the wireless network can be used to attack Bluetooth devices, such as the common Bluetooth DoS attack technology. To sum up, the existing attack technology is still likely to pose a threat to the blockchain cold wallet based on USB or Bluetooth communication.

7.2   Anti-interference QR Code Communication

The communication method used in this paper is based on QR Code, and the basic encoding process is shown in Fig. 6.

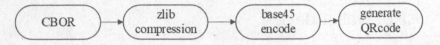

Fig. 6. QR Code encoding process. Zlib is a lossless data compression library, which is widely used in virtual hardware and operating systems.

The binary file is encoded as a Base45 file, similar to a Base64 file, but it uses only 45 characters [5]. A 17-byte text string in UTF-8 format, after being encoded as Base45, the amount of information becomes 29 bytes, and the Hex encoding result is 38 bytes. Compared to the existing Base64, Base32 and Base16 encodings, Base45 encoding provides a more compact encoding result. In this paper, it is used to compress binary encoded information to reduce redundant information in the subsequent QR Code generation process. CBOR is used for object signing and encryption which is a language similar to JSON but is actually a binary data form. The entire encoding and decoding process is implemented based on RUST. The specific process of each round of communication is: Device A encodes the information and generates a QR Code, which is displayed on the screen. Device B scans and identifies the code through the camera, performs background calculation and verification after obtaining the data, then generates a QR Code after the calculation is completed. Similarly, the code is displayed on the screen, and device A scans the code to obtain data information. The entire key signature process requires nine such information exchanges, and any round of information errors will terminate the key signature. Since the communication process is separated from traditional wireless technology and does not involve direct contact with hardware, this cold wallet device is a real network-separating device. The communication process is completely based on visible light, which is difficult for remote hackers or virus programs to attack the entire communication process, so the security is guaranteed. The multi-round interaction of GG18 signature scheme improves the signature security, but the nine-time scanning process also has a certain impact on the convenience when using the cold wallet. As mentioned in Sect. 2 of this paper, this hardware wallet is only enabled for signing in scenarios where the transaction amount is large. It is worth sacrificing some convenience.

7.3   Defense Against Electromagnetic Side-Channel Attacks

In addition to the attack methods carried out through the network, side channel attacks can also be used to attack hardware systems. Usually, side channel attack methods include electromagnetic attack method (DEMA) and energy attack method (DPA). Some malicious attackers can also directly damage wallet devices through electromagnetic pulses, which can result in serious consequences of key loss and asset loss. Mulder [8] performed DPA and DEMA attacks on the FPGA implementation of the GF-based elliptic cryptosystem, and it can be concluded from the experimental results that the DEMA attack method is more efficient. An electromagnetic shielding net made of conductive metal is placed inside the hardware wallet to defend against energy attacks, as shown in Fig. 7.

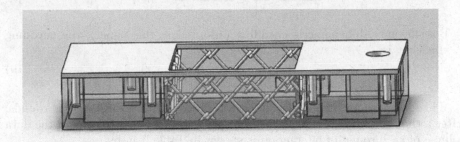

Fig. 7. Electromagnetic protection design, in which the metal net surrounds the computing devices.

When the conductive metal is interfered by the external magnetic field, the charge will temporarily move until the external magnetic field is offset by the internal magnetic field. In this case, the internal area of the metal is in a state of electrostatic shielding, which can effectively resist external electromagnetic pulse attacks. When the device is grounded, the internal magnetic field information will also become invisible.

8   Communication Efficiency of Cold Wallet

8.1   Comparison of Coding Efficiency

There are four main ways of QR Code encoding: pure numeric encoding, alphanumeric encoding (including 45 symbols such as numbers, capital letters, spaces, etc.), byte encoding, and language text encoding. This paper mainly explores the first three encoding methods. Since the default UTF-8 encoding cannot guarantee that each byte sequence has a corresponding codeword, a certain encoding method needs to be used in the process of generating a QR Code from a string of binary codes. Common binary encoding methods include hexadecimal encoding Hex, Base64, etc. The storage efficiency is defined as the ratio of the original information bit number to the encoded bit number. Therefore, from the perspective of storage, the larger the Base is, the higher the storage efficiency is. However, due to the limitation of the encoding method of QR code, the number of characters encoded in Base64 exceeds alphanumeric 45 characters, so only byte encoding can be used, which is consistent with the common computer representation, 8 bits per byte. While the Basic45 encoding can be used with alphanumeric encoding, and 5.5 bits is a byte, so the storage efficiency of the QR Code encoding schemes is as follows:

1) The default encoding method is Base64 plus Byte encoding, and the encoding efficiency is:

$$\frac{n}{\lceil \frac{n}{log_2 64} \times 8 \rceil} \approx \frac{n}{\frac{n}{log_2 64} \times 8} = 75\% \tag{18}$$

2) Base45 plus Alphanumeric encoding (adopted in this paper), the encoding efficiency is:

$$\frac{n}{\lceil \frac{n}{log_2 45} \times 5.5 \rceil} \approx \frac{n}{\frac{n}{log_2 45} \times 5.5} = 99.85\% \tag{19}$$

This paper adopts the GG18 signature scheme, with a total of nine rounds. After a thousand signature experiments, the average value is taken and the data volume of each round of interaction is shown in Table 1, in bytes.

Table 1. Message encoding length of each round.

Interactive rounds	1	2	3	4	5	6	7	8	9
Byte serialization	568	1732	57	98	40	617	40	156	57
Default serde_json string	1967	5677	148	287	117	1767	118	428	144
QR Code string	837	2194	59	113	60	585	60	165	59

In Table 1, the byte serialization length is the length of the original message of each round of interaction. Since the background is built based on RUST, the original message needs to be converted into the default string sequence using the default serde_json string conversion method of RUST programming language. Finally, the message should be encoded into the QR Code and scanned for communication. When the message is encoded into QR Code, the size of the QR Code bit stream is different due to the different encoding strategies. The coding method in this paper is compared with the default coding method, and the experimental results are shown in Fig. 8.

8.2 Optimization of Communication Process

Because this paper adopts the GG18 signature scheme, the data volume distribution of each round of interaction is non-uniform. As can be seen from Fig. 8 and Table 1, the data volume of the second round is abnormally large, reaching more than 2000 bytes. This round of huge data volume will greatly increase the requirements for hardware devices. It can be seen from the experimental results that the QR Code generated by the second round of data is very dense,

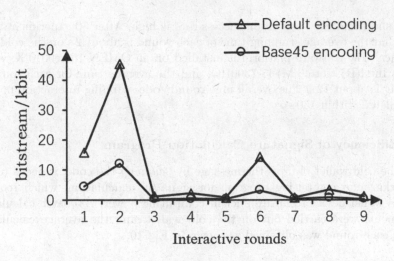

Fig. 8. Bitstream comparison of two encoding methods, in kilobits.

which requires the camera to have high resolution, and has strict requirements on ambient lighting, and the success rate of scanning the code is low. However, due to the small amount of data in other rounds, the generated QR Code is very sparse, as shown in Fig. 9. When scanning these sparse codes, the resolution requirements of the camera are quite simple, which will cause a serious waste of resources. Therefore, it is necessary to optimize interactive data volume in the second round.

Fig. 9. Comparison of QR Code images in different rounds. The left one is generated in round 2, the other in round 7.

The optimization strategy adopted: The data of the second round of GG18 interaction is divided into two sub-rounds. After scanning the two codes, the data of the two sub-rounds are spliced, and then sent to the background system for calculation. The data amount of each sub-cycle is reduced to 1000 bytes. Experiments show that even in dark lighting conditions, the camera with 5 million physical pixels can successfully complete the recognition, and the recognition time is short and the recognition success rate is high. After 50 experiments, it is found that the average scanning time of each round is about 2 s on the cold wallet device. The software platform is installed on an OMEN 15-ce001TX, whose CPU is Intel(R) Core(TM) i5-7300HQ, and the average time for each round of scanning is about 12 s. The overall nine-round code-scanning interaction process is completed within 150 s.

8.3   Efficiency of Signature Calculation Program

After the cold wallet obtains the message by scanning the code, it needs to call the background computing program for signature calculation, which requires the cold wallet device to have sufficient computing power. 100 batch calculation experiments were carried out on the cold wallet, and the average calculation time of each round was obtained as shown in Fig. 10.

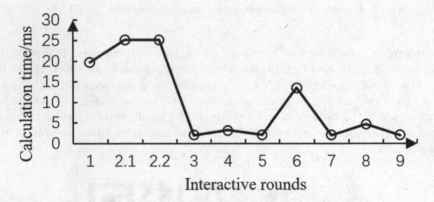

Fig. 10. Signing program running time per round.

It can be seen from the figure that each round of calculation time is not more than 30 ms, and the system signature calculation program efficiency can provide users with a smooth system experience.

9   Conclusion

The multi-party signature digital asset escrow system proposed in this paper adopts the threshold signature technology and homomorphic encryption algorithm to realize the GG18 multi-party signature scheme, effectively avoids the influence of single malicious party on digital currency transactions, and provides key retrieval service at the same time. In terms of key storage, a cold wallet communicating through QR Code is designed. The communication method ensures that the keys are completely stored isolated from network, and a defense method against electromagnetic side channel attacks is designed to improve the security of the cold wallet. The Base45 encoding scheme is adopted to optimize the process of code scanning and improve the communication efficiency of cold wallets.

The cold wallet designed in this paper sacrifices certain convenience in exchange for security. The follow-up work focuses on the lightweight design of hardware and the practice of the GG20 [11] multi-signature scheme, so as to improve the convenience of the escrow system on the premise of ensuring the existing security.

References

1. Acar, A., Aksu, H., Uluagac, A.S., Conti, M.: A survey on homomorphic encryption schemes: theory and implementation. ACM Comput. Surv. **51**(4), 1–35 (2018). https://doi.org/10.1145/3214303
2. Antonopoulos, A.M.: Mastering Bitcoin: Unlocking Digital Cryptocurrencies. O'Reilly Media, Inc. (2014)
3. Antonopoulos, A.M., Wood, G.: Mastering Ethereum: Building Smart Contracts and Dapps. O'reilly Media (2018)
4. Boneh, D., Gennaro, R., Goldfeder, S.: Using level-1 homomorphic encryption to improve threshold DSA signatures for bitcoin wallet security. In: Lange, T., Dunkelman, O. (eds.) LATINCRYPT 2017. LNCS, vol. 11368, pp. 352–377. Springer, Cham (2019). https://doi.org/10.1007/978-3-030-25283-0_19
5. Botta, M., Cavagnino, D.: A framework for reversible data embedding into base45 and other non-base64 encoded strings. Appl. Sci. **12**(1), 241 (2022). https://doi.org/10.3390/app12010241, https://www.mdpi.com/2076-3417/12/1/241
6. Canetti, R., Gennaro, R., Goldfeder, S., Makriyannis, N., Peled, U.: UC noninteractive, proactive, threshold ECDSA with identifiable aborts. In: Proceedings of the 2020 ACM SIGSAC Conference on Computer and Communications Security, CCS 2020, pp. 1769–1787. Association for Computing Machinery, New York (2020). https://doi.org/10.1145/3372297.3423367
7. Castagnos, G., Catalano, D., Laguillaumie, F., Savasta, F., Tucker, I.: Bandwidth-efficient threshold EC-DSA. In: Kiayias, A., Kohlweiss, M., Wallden, P., Zikas, V. (eds.) PKC 2020. LNCS, vol. 12111, pp. 266–296. Springer, Cham (2020). https://doi.org/10.1007/978-3-030-45388-6_10
8. De Mulder, E., Örs, S.B., Preneel, B., Verbauwhede, I.: Differential power and electromagnetic attacks on a FPGA implementation of elliptic curve cryptosystems. Comput. Electr. Eng. **33**(5–6), 367–382 (2007)
9. Ethereum, W.: Ethereum whitepaper. Ethereum (2014). https://ethereum.org. Accessed 07 July 2020
10. Gennaro, R., Goldfeder, S.: Fast multiparty threshold ECDSA with fast trustless setup. In: Proceedings of the 2018 ACM SIGSAC Conference on Computer and Communications Security, CCS 2018, pp. 1179–1194. Association for Computing Machinery, New York (2018). https://doi.org/10.1145/3243734.3243859
11. Gennaro, R., Goldfeder, S.: One round threshold ECDSA with identifiable abort. Cryptology ePrint Archive, Paper 2020/540 (2020). https://eprint.iacr.org/2020/540, https://eprint.iacr.org/2020/540
12. Gennaro, R., Goldfeder, S., Narayanan, A.: Threshold-optimal DSA/ECDSA signatures and an application to bitcoin wallet security. In: Manulis, M., Sadeghi, A.-R., Schneider, S. (eds.) ACNS 2016. LNCS, vol. 9696, pp. 156–174. Springer, Cham (2016). https://doi.org/10.1007/978-3-319-39555-5_9

13. Gennaro, R., Jarecki, S., Krawczyk, H., Rabin, T.: Robust threshold DSS signatures. Inf. Comput. **164**(1), 54–84 (2001). https://doi.org/10.1006/inco.2000.2881, https://www.sciencedirect.com/science/article/pii/S0890540100928815

14. Gennaro, R., Jarecki, S., Krawczyk, H., Rabin, T.: Robust threshold DSS signatures. In: Maurer, U. (ed.) EUROCRYPT 1996. LNCS, vol. 1070, pp. 354–371. Springer, Heidelberg (1996). https://doi.org/10.1007/3-540-68339-9_31

15. He, S., et al.: A social-network-based cryptocurrency wallet-management scheme. IEEE Access **6**, 7654–7663 (2018)

16. Ivanov, N., Yan, Q.: Ethclipper: a clipboard meddling attack on hardware wallets with address verification evasion. In: 2021 IEEE Conference on Communications and Network Security (CNS), pp. 191–199 (2021). https://doi.org/10.1109/CNS53000.2021.9705033

17. Kiffer, L., Rajaraman, R., shelat, A.: A better method to analyze blockchain consistency. In: Proceedings of the 2018 ACM SIGSAC Conference on Computer and Communications Security, CCS 2018, pp. 729–744. Association for Computing Machinery, New York (2018). https://doi.org/10.1145/3243734.3243814

18. Lindell, Y.: Fast secure two-party ECDSA signing. In: Katz, J., Shacham, H. (eds.) CRYPTO 2017. LNCS, vol. 10402, pp. 613–644. Springer, Cham (2017). https://doi.org/10.1007/978-3-319-63715-0_21

19. Lindell, Y., Nof, A.: Fast secure multiparty ECDSA with practical distributed key generation and applications to cryptocurrency custody. In: Proceedings of the 2018 ACM SIGSAC Conference on Computer and Communications Security, CCS 2018, pp. 1837–1854. Association for Computing Machinery, New York (2018). https://doi.org/10.1145/3243734.3243788

20. Lu, H.J., Liu, D.: An improved NFC device authentication protocol. PLOS One **16**(8), 1–8 (2021). https://doi.org/10.1371/journal.pone.0256367, https://doi.org/10.1371/journal.pone.0256367

21. Nakamoto, S.: Bitcoin: a peer-to-peer electronic cash system. Decentralized Bus. Rev. 21260 (2008)

22. Nissim, N., Yahalom, R., Elovici, Y.: USB-based attacks. Comput. Secur. **70**, 675–688 (2017). https://doi.org/10.1016/j.cose.2017.08.002, https://www.sciencedirect.com/science/article/pii/S0167404817301578

23. Pal, O., Alam, B., Thakur, V., Singh, S.: Key management for blockchain technology. ICT Express **7**(1), 76–80 (2021). https://doi.org/10.1016/j.icte.2019.08.002, https://www.sciencedirect.com/science/article/pii/S2405959519301894

24. Schindler, P., Judmayer, A., Stifter, N., Weippl, E.: EthDKG: distributed key generation with ethereum smart contracts. Cryptology ePrint Archive (2019)

25. Wang, Z., Ma, Z., Luo, S., Gao, H.: Key escrow protocol based on a tripartite authenticated key agreement and threshold cryptography. IEEE Access **7**, 149080–149096 (2019). https://doi.org/10.1109/ACCESS.2019.2946874

EthMB+: A Tamper-Proof Data Query Model Based on B+ Tree and Merkle Tree

Pengting Du, Yingjian Liu(✉), Yue Li, and Haoyu Yin

Ocean University of China, Qingdao 266100, People's Republic of China
liuyj@ouc.edu.cn

Abstract. The rise of cryptocurrencies has brought blockchain technology into wide focus. Because of its immutable, traceable and consistent protocol, it provides a new solution for trusted data storage and decentralized computing. Most existing blockchain systems store blockchain data in key-value databases with simple semantic descriptions. However, the data storage system only provides a single query mode and limited query types. As a result, it is impossible to carry out effective data analysis and mining on the ever-increasing data in the blockchain system. To expand the data query function of the blockchain system, the data in the maintenance system must not be tampered with. This paper proposes a tamper-proof data query model (EthMB+) based on B+ tree and Merkle tree to ensure users get correct query results. EthMB+ reconstructs the organization by extracting part of the blockchain data and then inserting them into the MB+ tree structure. The query method is designed based on the structure of MB+ tree. Experimental results show that EthMB+ has good usability.

Keywords: Blockchain · Ethereum · MB+ tree · Data query

1 Introduction

Blockchain is a core supporting technology of hot bitcoin in recent years [1]. In essence, a blockchain encapsulates generated data into a chained block data structure sorted in chronological order. This structure only supports appending, not tampering. In a blockchain system, all nodes participating in the blockchain network maintain a shared ledger, and each node keeps a copy of the ledger's data. At present, blockchain technology has been applied in many fields. The research of blockchain technology is still in its initial stage. If we can achieve more efficient data organization and richer data queries while maintaining the characteristics of blockchain system and data itself, then this technology will bring new changes in various industries.

Query optimization is based on external database. EtherQL [2] added a query layer in the public blockchain system to solve the problem of its insufficient data query capability. Data on the chains were copied to MongoDB [3], an off-chain associated database, to assist the blockchain system in data query. F. Aprama and K. Utijarsa [4] enhanced and extended the query functions defined in EtherQL, further improving the usability of blockchain technology among users and developers. VQL [5] designed a verifiable query

© The Author(s), under exclusive license to Springer Nature Singapore Pte Ltd. 2022
Y. Sun et al. (Eds.): CBCC 2022, CCIS 1736, pp. 49–59, 2022.
https://doi.org/10.1007/978-981-19-8877-6_4

layer that could provide efficient query services and trusted query results for blockchain-based systems. A. Bracciali et al. [6] and H. Keloder et al. [7] proposed to synchronize blockchain data with local databases and then analyze the data.

Query optimization is also based on built-in structure. S. Hu et al. [8], Sven Helmer et al. [9] and P. Ruan et al. [10] all utilized the smart contract built into the blockchain system to expand its query capability. VChain [11] designed a verifiable query framework to be used on the blockchain. It was an accumulator-based data structure that authenticated and dynamically aggregated properties to be queried. Gem^2-tree [12] further designed a new gas-efficient verifiable data structure for verifiable processing under the hybrid storage framework. In order to improve the efficiency of blockchain tracking new data, X. Liu et al. [13] designed and proposed a data tracking method based on LevelDB. This method can query the newly updated data in memory with only consuming a small amount of space.

This paper proposes a solution to the query problem of blockchain data. Using Ethereum as the experimental platform, we propose a tamper-proof data query model – EthMB+ based on B+ tree and Merkle tree. Our main contributions are as follows: (1) EthMB+ is built to organize Ethereum blockchain data. (2) Based on EthMB+, key-value query and range query are proposed to support the query of Ethereum blockchain data. (3) The effectiveness of the proposed method is verified by experiments.

2 Preliminaries

This section describes blockchain-related technologies.

2.1 Ethereum

Ethereum has become the most popular public blockchain platform and is considered as a symbol of the Blockchain 2.0 era. It is built in a Turing-complete programming language that allows users to write contracts. Currently, Ethereum's development team is trying to improve the scalability of the system by using sharding technology because more and more nodes are involved. However, the current cryptocurrency-based segmentation scheme cannot adapt to the smart contract system introduced by Ethereum. Cross-transaction and data interaction are also difficult to some extent. The overall architecture of Ethereum can be divided into core layer, service layer and application layer.

2.2 Blockchain Organization

Although different blockchain systems differ in their specific structures due to different application scenarios, the underlying data organization and storage modules are similar. The data organization storage module is mainly responsible for the preservation of chain data, and the coding and decoding of chain data and access.

A complete block is divided into two parts, i.e., block header and block body. In general, block header contains more information. Blockchain is composed of blocks linked by encrypted hash pointers. There are certain differences among blocks in different blockchain systems. We describe the data structure of block in Ethereum in detail.

The block header contains: ParentHash and UncleHash (hash values for the previous block and uncle block), Coinbase (the address of the miner who excavated the block), StateRoot (the root of account state trie), ReceiptsRoot (hash value of transaction receipt), TransRoot (the Merkle root node generated by the transactions in this block), GasLimit (the allowed Gas consumption), GasUsed (Gas used by all transactions in the block), Number (the height of block), Timestamp (the time of the block being mined), Difficulty (difficulty of mining), Nonce (the calibration value). Block body includes the collection of transactions, and the collection of tertiary bulks. Ethereum maintains transactions in the current block, receipt information after transactions, and the state of accounts in the system using three modified MPT trees (i.e., transaction tree, receipt tree, and state tree).

3 EthMB+ Description

In Sect. 2, we explain how blockchain data is organized and how Ethereum works. To meet users' query needs, Ethereum provides some query-related APIs. But these APIs can only query a single block or transaction at a time, which is inefficient. While expanding the query function of blockchain system, it should also ensure not to destroy the characteristics of blockchain data themselves. Based on this, we propose EthMB+ (see Fig. 1), a tamper-proof data query model based on B+ tree and Merkle tree. EthMB+ model involves three parties. One is the blockchain system, as a distributed database to store data. The second one is to reorganize the MB+ tree structure of blockchain data. And the last one is to provide users with data query service. The model is divided into three parts: data extraction, MB+ index, and query method.

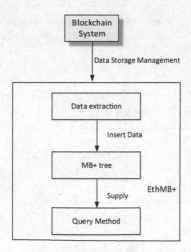

Fig. 1. EthMB+ structure.

3.1 MB+ Tree

Although indexes can greatly improve the efficiency of data retrieval, they increase the consumption of storage space. When the amount of data to be retrieved is large, this consumption is particularly obvious because the volume of index structures formed is also large. It is impossible to store all such index structures in memory. In a practical application scenario, the index is generally in the form of files stored in the equipment of the disk. Therefore, the index of retrieval including index structure itself is retrieved, and disk I/O operation two aspects. Since the data field of the B+ tree only appears in the leaf node, the query of the data value corresponding to a key value can only be completed by retrieving the target leaf node from the root node. Connected leaf nodes greatly enhance the accessibility of interval search. Generally, the leaf nodes of B+ trees are stored sequentially in disk. When a value is read, the disk prefetch will read the contiguous data into memory in advance, which improves the efficiency of B+ tree range query.

Merkle tree is a kind of tree structure designed and proposed by Ralph Merkle, a scientist in computer field, in 1979. It is also called hash binary tree. The tree has three types of nodes: root node, intermediate node, and leaf node. The leaf node stores the original data value, and the non-leaf node stores the hash value of its child node, which can be calculated by using various hash algorithms such as SHA1 and SHA256.

To ensure that blockchain data will not be tampered with and to expand the data query capability of blockchain system, we combined the characteristics of B+ tree and Merkle tree to design MB+ tree. MB+ tree organizes and constructs blockchain data according to B+ tree indexes. In the construction process, according to the Merkle tree principle, hash operation is carried out on the block chain data to achieve the immutability of data and index. Figure 2 shows the structure of the MB+ tree.

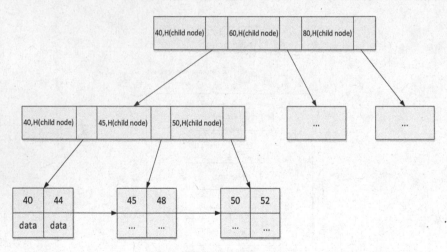

Fig. 2. MB+ tree.

3.2 Blockchain Data Extraction and Insertion

Ethereum provides some APIs for users to perform simple data query operations. The EthMB+ model uses a similar approach to access block data and transaction information stored in the blockchain, decoding and extracting the data needed for model construction for later use. The EthMB+ model takes block data and transaction information from the underlying blockchain system reorganizes and initializes this data, and inserts the data into the MB+ tree. The specific steps are as follows:

- Step 1: find the target leaf node according to the key value of the data to be inserted. That is, find the insertion position and insert the data into the target leaf node. If no root node exists, a leaf node is created to hold the key and data values. Then create an intermediate node and set the leaf node to be the child of that intermediate node. The key value to be inserted and the hash value of the child node is stored in the middle node. The middle node is taken as the root node. The insertion operation is complete. If the root node is empty, a leaf node is created to hold the key and data values of the data to be inserted. Set the leaf node as the child node of the root node, save the key value and the hash value of the child node to the root node, and complete the single insertion. If there is a root node and it is not empty, the key value in the root node is compared with the key value of the data record to be inserted, and the child node that meets the requirements is loaded according to the comparison result. Repeat this process until the target leaf node is loaded and the blockchain data is inserted into it, and the single insertion is complete.
- Step 2: adjust to the MB+ tree. Check whether the capacity of the leaf node after data insertion exceeds the upper limit. If not, the adjustment ends at this point. If the capacity limit is exceeded, nodes need to be split. Create a new leaf node, insert part of the split content in the node list into the new leaf node, define the leaf node as the child node of the middle node in the upper layer, and add it to the linked list formed by the original leaf nodes. Continue to overrun detection capacity. The parent node to split operation beyond the capacity of the intermediate node. In this process, the hash value of child node should be updated in time. This step is repeated until all the nodes in the MB+ tree have limited capacity, and the whole tree structure keeps equilibrium. Then, the adjustment ends.
- Step 3: save the adjustment of MB+ tree. The data list stored on a single node is stored as a whole. The pointer relation between nodes is retained. The entire MB+ tree structure is RLP encoded and stored on the local device. This operation greatly reduces storage space consumption and further improves data security. To reduce the storage space occupied by MB+ tree structure, the EthMB+ model extracts some data from the blockchain system for model construction according to user requirements, which occupies less storage space. In addition to providing efficient data query methods, the EthMB+ model ensures data correctness through its own tamperproof mechanism.

3.3 Blockchain Data Query

EthMB+ supports key and range queries for blockchain data. For the key-value query, the query method only supports the input of a single parameter. If two parameters are entered, an error message will be displayed. While for the range query, it is the opposite, which further realizes the standardization of the data query method.

Key-Value Query. When the key-value query method is called and a single parameter is entered, the search starts from the root node of the MB+ tree. This key value is compared to the list of key values in the root node. The child nodes loaded from disk are selected based on the comparison results, and the comparison continues, repeating the process until the search is locked to the target leaf node. If a key value equal to the input parameter exists in the target leaf node, the query succeeds, and the corresponding data value of the key value. Otherwise, data corresponding to input parameters does not exist in the current model. As the amount of inserted data increases, the MB+ tree uses more and more storage space. When querying, it is unnecessary and uneconomical to load the entire MB+ tree structure into memory at once. Therefore, the EthMB+ model only loads one node into the memory during the operation to compare with the input parameters, and selects the next node to load according to the comparison results. The loading process stops until the leaf node is successfully loaded into the memory.

Range Query. MB+ trees retain the B+ tree leaf nodes linked from beginning to end, so range query can be implemented by traversing a linked list of leaf nodes. In response to the user's query request, the model loads the leftmost leaf node from the local disk to the memory. The key value list in this node is retrieved, and the data value corresponding to the key value that meets the requirements is added to the tolt set. After the retrieval is completed, the next leaf node is loaded. Since the key values within and between nodes in the linked list of leaf nodes are all arranged in order. In the process of loading nodes and comparing key values, once a key value the right boundary of the interval appears, the value will be discarded and the current result set will be returned, and the query ends.

Data Validation. The blockchain system is constantly generating new blocks, with more and more data. If the new data is extracted and merged into the EthMB+ model once generated, the system may be overloaded with disk I/O operations and the efficiency of the model will be affected. Therefore, the EthMB+ model periodically bundles a portion of newly generated blockchain data and merges it into the MB+ tree. After the insertion is complete, the model copies the latest root value in memory so that there are two backups of the latest root value on disk and in memory. Each call to the MB+ tree produces a comparison between the root node in memory and the root node on disk. If there is an inconsistency, the data has changed. In this way, not only can users check the correctness of data synchronously when they query data, but also the correctness of data can be checked when the model is updated periodically. Such tamper tamper-proof low cost and easy to operate.

In addition, EthMB+ model also provides a path to a particular value in a model authentication models validation paths to specific values based on the properties of Merkle trees, allowing users to validate specific values based on a small amount of information. The principle is that the value stored in the verification path of a specific value is hashed from bottom to top until the root node is calculated. The obtained root node value is compared with the original value stored to verify the correctness of a specific value. The specific algorithm is as follows:

Algorithm 1 Data verification based on the validation path.

Input: Unproven value, Verify the path, root-hash;
Output: true or false;
1: hash = Hash (value);
2: **while** path.pop () is not null
//Take the path value from bottom up
3:   hash = **Hash** (hash.path.pop ());
4: **end**;
5: **if** hash == root-hash **then**
6:   **return** true;
7: **end**;
8: **return** false;

---

4 Implementation and Evaluation

The experimental hardware environment adopted in this paper is a PC with Windows10 operating system, whose basic configuration is Intel (R) Core (TM) i5-6500cpu and 16 GB RAM. The PC runs EthMB+ and accesses the test network Rinkeby through the Geth client of Ethereum to obtain the dataset used in the experiment. In order to evaluate the performance of EthMB+, EthMB+ is set up to perform experiments on multiple datasets with different data volumes and record the results. The data volume of the experimental dataset from small to large are respectively 100,000, 300,000, 500,000, 700,000, 900,000, 1.1 million, 1.3 million, 1.5 million, 1.7 million, 1.9 million, 2.1 million, 2.3 million and 2.5 million. EthMB+ model decodes and extracts blockchain data to obtain the dataset required by the experiment. In this paper, the transaction value is selected as the key value, the Gas value consumed by the transaction, the block number of the block where the transaction is encapsulated, and the identifier of the transaction in the block are taken as the data value. The data attributes are shown in Table 1. Ethereum is a commonly used application development platform. Transaction data is the key data with a large amount of data in Ethereum, which is more representative as experimental data.

Table 1. Data attributes of the dataset.

Key-value	Transaction value
Data value filed	Gas used of transaction
	Block number
	Transaction identifier of block

4.1 Storage Usage

EthMB+ model calls Ethereum's built-in API to access blockchain data. According to the data attributes set, the corresponding dataset is extracted through decoding. The access extraction process is traversed from the first block until the threshold block is traversed. After building the MB+ tree, the index structure of the MB+ tree is encoded into the device where the model resides. After this step, part of the storage space will be consumed. The usage of storage space is shown in Fig. 3. As the number of blocks involved in model construction increases, the consumption of storage space becomes larger and faster. But this storage consumption is tiny compared to the overall storage footprint of blockchain data. According to statistical data and experimental results, when the block data volume reaches 2.5 million, the storage space will be occupied about 20 GB, while the storage space occupied by EthMB+ model is less than 800 MB. This shows that the EthMB+ model performs better in terms of storage performance.

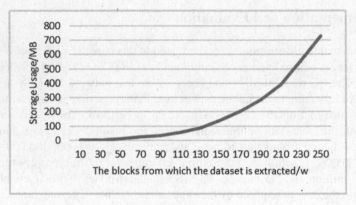

Fig. 3. Storage space.

4.2 Insertion Performance

EthMB+ model requires that the transaction value dataset be constructed and inserted into MB+ tree for subsequent query. The construction process involves data insertion into MB+ tree node and node hash value calculation, which are carried out synchronically. After insertion, a copy of the root node of the MB+ tree is stored in memory for verification. The constructed MB+ tree was encoded by RLP and saved. Figure 4 shows the total time required to build and store an MB+ tree in a dataset with different data volumes. As can be seen from the figure, the time to build MB+ tree increases with the number of blocks increasing. Figure 5 records the time required to insert a single piece of data into the model with different data volumes. As can be seen from the figure, the insertion time of single data decreases and tends to be stable with the increase of block number. There is a significant downward trend in the number of blocks from 100,000 to 300,000, due to fewer users and nodes initially participating in the Ethereum blockchain. Although new blocks are constantly being generated, there is a certain gap between the growth rate of the number of transactions and the speed of the block generation, which is reflected in the average single record time will be slightly longer. The second half of the image shows that the insertion time of a single record is relatively short and tends to be stable.

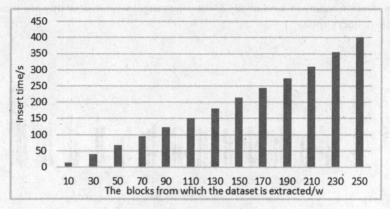

Fig. 4. Dataset insertion time.

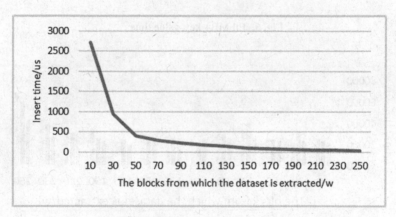

Fig. 5. Single data insertion time.

4.3 Query Performance

After the MB+ tree is constructed, the EthMB+ model provides users with key-value query and range query. Figure 6 records the experimental results of the key-value query. The experiment tests the query time by inputting different parameters in the same dataset. As can be seen from the figure, when the number of blocks increases, the time consumed for querying key values rises slowly. On the whole, the EthMB+ model has a good and stable query time for key-value.

Figure 7 records the range query results EthMB+ model, the figure shows that with the rising numbers involved in the model building blocks, the scope of the query time slowly rising trend. On the whole, this is due to the more involved in the model building blocks, eventually participate in MB+ tree to build the more data, then construct a complete tree structure contains the number of leaf nodes will increase. In general, the time required for range query remains in a relatively short time range, with a slow upward trend and a good range query time.

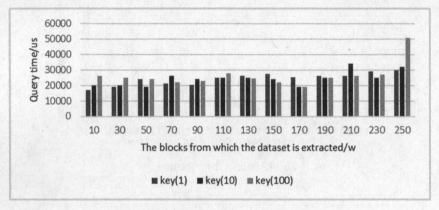

Fig. 6. EthMB+ key-value time.

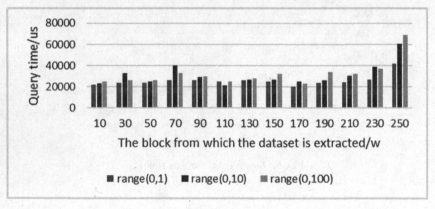

Fig. 7. EthMB+ range time.

5 Conclusion

To expand the query function of blockchain system, and consider the reorganization of blockchain data while maintaining it not to be tampered with, this paper proposes a tamper-proof data query model (EthMB+) based on B+ tree and Merkle tree. We briefly introduce the reorganization construction of its overall architecture around blockchain data query optimization design and analyze the principle and process of EthMB+ model. We then evaluated the storage, insertion, and query performance of EthMB+ model. Experimental results show that EthMB+ model has good performance in all aspects.

Acknowledgments. This work was supported partially by the National Natural Science Foundation of China under Grant No. 62172378, No. 61572448, No. 61673357, No. 61827810, and by the National Key R&D Program of China under Grant No. 2020YFB1707701.

References

1. Nakamoto, S.: Bitcoin: A Peer-to-Peer Electronic Cash System. White Paper (2008)
2. Li, Y., Zheng, K., Yan, Y., Liu, Q., Zhou, X.: EtherQL: a query layer for blockchain system. In: Candan, S., Chen, L., Pedersen, T.B., Chang, L., Hua, W. (eds.) DASFAA 2017. LNCS, vol. 10178, pp. 556–567. Springer, Cham (2017). https://doi.org/10.1007/978-3-319-55699-4_34
3. MongoDB. MongoDB Documentation [EB/OL]. https://docs.mongodb.com/
4. Pratama, F.A., Mutijarsa, K.: Query support for data processing and analysis on ethereum blockchain. In: 2018 International Symposium on Electronics and Smart Devices (ISESD), Bandung, pp. 1–5 (2018)
5. Peng, Z., Wu, H., Xiao, B., Guo, S.: VQL: providing query efficiency and data authenticity in blockchain systems. In: 2019 IEEE 35th International Conference on Data Engineering Workshops (ICDEW), Macao, Macao, pp. 1–6 (2019)
6. Bartoletti, M., Bracciali, A., Lande, S., Pompianu, L.: A general framework for blockchain analytics (2017). http://arxiv.org/abs/1707.01021. Accessed 08 May
7. Kalodner, H., Goldfeder, S., Chator, A., Möser, M., Narayanan, A.: BlockSci: design and applications of a blockchain analysis platform (2017). http://arxiv.org/abs/1709.02489. Accessed 08 May
8. Hu, S., Cai, C., Wang, Q., Wang, C., Luo, X., Ren, K.: Searching an encrypted cloud meets blockchain: a decentralized, reliable and fair realization. In: IEEE Conference on Computer Communications, IEEE INFOCOM 2018, Honolulu, HI, pp. 792–800 (2018)
9. Helmer, S., Roggia, M., Ioini, N.E., Pahl, C.: EthernityDB – integrating database functionality into a blockchain. In: Benczúr, A., et al. (eds.) ADBIS 2018. CCIS, vol. 909, pp. 37–44. Springer, Cham (2018). https://doi.org/10.1007/978-3-030-00063-9_5
10. Ruan, P., Chen, G., Dinh, T.T.A., Lin, Q., Ooi, B., Zhang, M.: Fine-grained, secure and efficient data provenance on blockchain systems. Proc. VLDB Endow. **12**(9), 975–988 (2019)
11. Xu, C., Zhang, C., Xu, J.: vChain: enabling verifiable boolean range queries over blockchain databases. In: Proceedings of the 2019 International Conference on Management of Data, Amsterdam Netherlands, pp. 141–158 (2019)
12. Zhang, C., Xu, C., Xu, J., Tang, Y., Choi, B.: GEM^2-Tree: a gas-efficient structure for authenticated range queries in blockchain. In: 2019 IEEE 35th International Conference on Data Engineering (ICDE), Macao, Macao, pp. 842–853 (2019)
13. Liu, X., Yu, X., Ma, X., Kuang, H.: A method to improve the fresh data query efficiency of blockchain. In: 2020 12th International Conference on Measuring Technology and Mechatronics Automation (ICMTMA), Phuket, Thailand, pp. 823–827 (2020)

Overview of Zero-Knowledge Proof and Its Applications in Blockchain

Yu Zhou, Zeming Wei, Shansi Ma, and Hua Tang[✉]

South China Normal University, Guangzhou 510632, China
tanghua@scnu.edu.cn

Abstract. The rapid development of blockchain technology applications and the increased demand for data security has greatly driven the research on privacy protection. Zero-knowledge proof is a method that can be used to verify the correctness of data while allowing the provers not to reveal confidential information. In this paper, we first sort out the development process of zero-knowledge proofs, classify them from a model perspective and compare the performance of various protocols. Then we explore the applications of zero-knowledge proofs in privacy transactions and scaling in blockchain and analyze them with specific application cases. Finally, we analyze and summarize the trends of zero-knowledge proofs and provide an appropriate outlook on future improvement directions.

Keywords: Zero-knowledge proofs · Blockchain · NIZK · CRS · SNARK · STARK · MPC-in-the-head

1 Introduction

Blockchain is a peer-to-peer distributed ledger technology based on cryptographic algorithms that record all transaction data on all historical blockchains. Generally speaking, transaction data, including transaction amount, account address and account balance, should be private information of individuals. However, due to the transparent and open nature of blockchain, supplemented by statistical methods such as sociological and data mining, these transactions may face the threat of privacy leakage. Therefore, privacy protection has become a hot topic in the current blockchain technology research.

Although users of blockchains can hide user information through wallet addresses, security and privacy on blockchains are not without problems [43, 44]. For example, sender and recipient addresses and transaction amounts are publicly available, and the analysis of big data may expose the connection to physical users. Several cryptographic approaches exist, including homomorphic encryption, ring signature, secure multiparty computation, and zero-knowledge proof. Homomorphic encryption supports certain types of operations on ciphertexts without decryption. It can be used to secure account balances and transaction amounts. Unfortunately, it does not secure account addresses. A ring signature is a special digital signature that does not reveal who has signed it. A ring signature can be used to secure an account address. However, it does

Y. Sun et al. (Eds.): CBCC 2022, CCIS 1736, pp. 60–82, 2022.
https://doi.org/10.1007/978-981-19-8877-6_5

not guarantee the security of account balances and transaction amounts. Secure Multiparty Computation is a cryptographic protocol that distributes computation tasks to multiple participants, where different participants cannot know the data of other participants. It secures account balances and transaction amounts but does not secure account addresses. In addition, homomorphic encryption, ring signature and secure multiparty computation cannot be used to verify that sufficient transaction amounts are available for legitimate transactions without revealing transaction coins, account addresses, and account balances. Zero-knowledge proof is a cryptographic protocol used to verify a claim's veracity or knowledge of a secret value without disclosing anything other than the prover's knowledge of these things.

Goldwasser, Micali, and Rackoff first introduced the concept of zero-knowledge proofs [1] in 1985, initiating an important branch of cryptographic theory. The greatest property of zero-knowledge proofs that distinguishes them from other cryptographic theories is that they allow the provers to convince the verifier of the correctness of a statement without revealing any other knowledge. Zero-knowledge proof is a powerful cryptographic tool, and it needs to satisfy three properties:

- **Completeness:** Given a statement and a witness, the prover can convince the verifier.
- **Soundness:** A malicious prover cannot convince the verifier of a false statement.
- **Zero-knowledge:** The proof does not reveal anything but the truth of the statement; in particular, it does not reveal the prover's witness.

Zero-knowledge proof technology can be used to break many of the limitations of privacy and data security issues, which are needed urgently in blockchain applications. In a sense, blockchain and zero-knowledge proofs are a perfect match. Introducing zero-knowledge proofs on the blockchain can reasonably resolve the contradiction between encryption and public verifiability and play an important role in solving data security, privacy security, and regulatory oversight issues.

Early zero-knowledge proofs can be divided into interactive zero-knowledge proof protocols and non-interactive zero-knowledge proofs. Interactive zero-knowledge proof protocols were the starting point of zero-knowledge proof technology. Interactive zero-knowledge proofs allow interaction between the individual proving their knowledge and the individual validating the proof. In such a system, the prover can reveal to the individual with whom he/her interacts, but somebody who merely observes you may not be able to verify your claim.

With in-depth research on zero-knowledge proof protocols, Blum et al. [2] first proposed the Common Reference String (CRS) model to extend the zero-knowledge proof system to a non-interactive zero-knowledge (NIZK) proof system. Unlike previous interactive proofs, a non-interactive zero-knowledge proof system only contains messages sent by the prover to the verifier, and then the verifier can verify it. After that, comprehensive research on the CRS and NIZK proof system started properly. The generic reference string model is commonly used in non-interactive zero-knowledge proof systems.

With the interaction problem solved, the next goal is to make NIZKs more efficient and concise. There are increasingly stringent requirements on the communication complexity and verification efficiency of NIZKs. As a result, the concept of Zero-knowledge Succinct Non-interactive Arguments of Knowledge (zk-SNARKs) has emerged and been widely studied, becoming one of the most important parts of the modern cryptography field. Unfortunately, zk-SNARKs require a trusted setup, which refers to the initial creation event of the keys used to create the proofs required for personal statements and the verification of those proofs. The reliance on a trusted set-up has been one of the largest areas of concern for critics of SNARKs. In addition, these initial settings of zk-SNARK are circuit-specific one-time trusted initial settings, i.e., the CRS generated by this initial setting can only be targeted to a specific circuit and not to an arbitrary circuit. To address these issues, cryptographers have made a series of studies and new lines of research, such as universal updatable zk-SNARKs, transparent zk-SNARKs and MPC-in-the-head, which we will discuss in Sects. 4–6.

To summarize the above technologies, we believe it is necessary to study zero-knowledge proof systems from the development process perspective, communication complexity, efficiency and security. To this end, we make three contributions:

1. We sort out and classify the development process of zero-knowledge proof and summarize each stage's related technologies. We explore the applications of zero-knowledge proofs in privacy transactions and scaling in blockchain and analyze them with specific application cases.
2. We compare different technologies of zero-knowledge proof from the technical point of view of communication complexity, efficiency, and security and point out the technical challenges to be solved.
3. We explore the latest technologies and put forward the law and trend of the future development and evolution of the zero-knowledge proof system.

This research paper is organized as follows: In Sect. 2, we describe a lineage of the development of early zero-knowledge proofs, including interactive zero-knowledge proofs and non-interactive zero-knowledge proofs. Sections introduce the features and related studies of zk-SNARKs based on CRS. In Sects. 4–6, we present several improvement options for the traditional CRS model, including universal updatable zk-SNARKs, transparent zk-SNARK and ZKP based on MPC-in-the-head. Section 7 outlines the application of zero-knowledge proofs in blockchain and introduces specific use cases. Finally, we predict future research directions and challenges for zero-knowledge proofs in Sect. 8 and conclude this paper in Sect. 9.

2 First Zero-Knowledge Proofs

2.1 Interactive Zero-Knowledge Proofs

The earliest zero-knowledge proof systems came from Interactive Zero-Knowledge (IZK) proofs protocols. Interactive zero-knowledge proof systems allow interactions between two communicating parties or any computer system without revealing knowledge. The prover can interact with the verifier multiple times, and the verifier reduces the probability of cheating the prover to a very small value by repeated challenges. As a result, the prover can prove the knowledge, and the validator can validate it.

In general, an interactive zero-knowledge proof works as follows:

- The prover sends a witness to the verifier. The witness works as a commitment in the protocol.
- The verifier sends a challenge back to the prover. The challenge could be in the form of random inspections.
- The prover sends a response to the verifier.
- The verifier checks if the response is correct.

After Goldwasser et al. [1] introduced the concept of zero-knowledge proofs in 1985, Gilles Brassard et al. [3] gave a general perfect zero-knowledge interaction proof for NPs in 1986, which does not rely on unproven cryptographic assumptions. Goldwasser et al. [4] suggested that in interactive proofs, verifiers should accept correct proofs and reject false assertions with at least 2/3 probability. Nevertheless, applications often do not tolerate a one-third error rate, so the security rate must be amplified.

Boyer et al. [5] improved the interactive zero-knowledge proof system by reducing the communication complexity, achieving a probability of undetected cheating below 2^{-k} with an expensive initialization process where k is an adjustable security parameter. The work of Boyer et al. reduced the error rate of the interactive zero-knowledge proof system, but the communication between the interacting parties remained complex.

In 1990, a well-known complexity theory theorem was proved, called the Probabilistically Checkable Proofs (PCP) theorem [22–24]. PCP theorem stated that NP assertions have probabilistically verifiable proofs that can be verified in normal proof size and log polynomial time. The emergence of PCP has inspired the study of zero-knowledge proofs, providing a new approach to them.

In 1992, based on the PCP theorem and inspired by Boyer [5], Killian [6] proposed the first sublinear zero-knowledge argumentation system. In this paper, Killian presented new zero-knowledge interactive proofs and arguments for languages in NP. With the same error probability as the work of Boyer et al., Killian's zero-knowledge proof system requires only logarithmic order of communication size and verification time. It was also the first succinct proof system in history, whose argument system with communication size is smaller than the statement's size.

Killian gave the first zero-knowledge proof with a sublinear communication scale and verification time. However, in Killian's scheme, at least four rounds of interaction between the provers and verifiers were required, which was not of high application value. For cryptographic applications, non-interactive zero-knowledge proofs are more meaningful.

2.2 Non-interactive Zero-Knowledge Proofs

Although interactive proofs may work well in some cases, it is clear that there are some problems, such as possible collusion between the provers and verifiers, bystanders may not be able to believe the proofs during the interaction fully, and the interaction of communication may bring additional attacks. Considering the shortcomings of interactive zero-knowledge proofs and their increased application requirements, researchers are not satisfied with zero-knowledge proof systems that require interaction between two parties. As a result, Non-Interactive Zero-Knowledge Proofs (NIZK) was born.

NIZK is a further development of zero-knowledge proof theory, where the verifier does not need to interact with the prover to check that the witness is correct. In a non-interactive zero-knowledge proof system, the verifier does not need to reply to the prover. That is, in an interactive zero-knowledge proof system, there is only one message that is sent from the prover to the verifier.

In general, a non-interactive zero-knowledge proof works as follows:

- The prover generates a witness.
- The prover takes the witness and other necessary information as inputs and outputs the challenge using some hash function.
- The prover calculates the response and then sends the witness, the challenge, and the response to the verifier.

The security of NIZK is based on the fact that validators cannot predict the outcome of a hash function.

In 1988, Blum [2] introduced the concept of the Common Reference String (CRS) model and gave the first NIZK proof system for NP language based on the CRS. He pointed out that interactions in an interactive zero-knowledge proof can be replaced by sharing a common random shout string. CRS is based on the assumption that both the prover and the verifier have the same reference string. A third party may randomly generate the CRS, or it may be the output of a function. The important thing is that the two parties who complete the protocol do not know how the string is generated. Compared with the interactive zero-knowledge proof system, the CRS model relies on the randomness of strings and has stronger practicality.

Although Blum proposed the CRS model to extend interactive zero-knowledge proofs to non-interactive zero-knowledge proofs, he did not consider NIZK proof systems to be a substitute for all IZK proof systems at the beginning, and he also considered the CRS model to be weaker than the interactive model. Then, the research of turning interactive zero-knowledge proofs into NIZK arguments gradually began.

Fiat and Shamir found a way to transform an interactive protocol into a non-interactive one through the "Fiat-Shamir Heuristic" approach. The emergence of the "Fiat-Shamir Heuristic" reduced the communication complexity of non-interactive zero-knowledge proof systems, and the practicality of non-interactive zero-knowledge proof systems was greatly enhanced. Then, NIZK became more popular, and more research focused on this direction.

Feige et al. [10] showed how to construct NIZK proofs based on one-way permutations or certified trap permutations, which was the first NIZK proof system based on general assumptions. Blum [11] constructed the first computational NIZK proof system for multiple theorems. Shamir [12] presented the first publicly verifiable NIZK based on the one-way alignment assumption. Damgård [13] improved [20] by designing a circuit-satisfiability NIZK proof system that can prove an arbitrary NP statement non-interactively. Also, he proposed a protocol based on tables within collisions, which makes the construction of NIZK for NP problems more straightforward.

The problem of transforming from an interactive zero-knowledge proof system to a NIZK proof system has been largely solved. The next goal was to construct efficient NIZK proofs. At that time, the popular method was called the "hidden random bits" model, which hides random bits in the CRS. This model assumes that the prover has a string of random bits unknown to the verifier. The prover convinces the verifier of the truth of the statement in question by revealing a subset of these bits and keeping the rest secret.

The difference between the hidden bit model and the CRS model is that the verifier can only see part of the CRS, while the prover can decide which part of the CRS the verifier sees.

The hidden bit model could be instantiated in the standard model under well-studied assumptions.

Hidden random bit models can be instantiated in the standard model. With this model, Feige et al. [10] successfully enabled the provers of polynomials to prove polynomial theorems based on a single random string in written form under general assumptions. Inspired by the work in [10], Kilian presented a NIZK-proof system for SAT based on One-Way Permutation. In this paper, $O(n\log^c nk)$ bits were hidden, and in Kilian's subsequent work [14], this number was reduced to $(n\log(n/\varepsilon)k)$.

Another way to make the NIZK argumentation system efficient and feasible is to construct efficient but heuristically secure proof systems [13, 54, 72, 93]. DeSantis et al. [15] discuss the length of CRS in NIZK and shows a NIZK proof system for NP problems with a CRS of length $\Theta(ne + \log(1/s))$, where $e > 0$ is a constant and s is a reasonable error bound. Subsequently, more and more studies focused on this direction with fruitful results. [17, 74] proposed a non-interactive zero-knowledge proof technique based on bilinear mappings and the first perfect NIZK argument system for any NP language. In their system, the size of the CRS is $O(k)$, where k is a security parameter, and thus it is independent of the size of the NP statement. Immediately after, in 2008, Groth et al. proposed an efficient framework for pairing-based NIZK, whose security is essentially based on any standard assumptions about pairing-friendly groups, creating a new research direction for applying NIZK.

In conclusion, NIZK has solved two problems from its emergence to its development: one is to transform IZK into NIZK, and the other is to continuously optimize NIZK and build a more efficient and concise argument system to make it more practical. Simplicity and efficiency are also the core ideas of zk-SNARKs.

3   Zk-SNARKs Based on CRS

The earliest Succinct proofs system was proposed by Kilian [6], based on PCP, through four rounds of interaction. With continuous research on reducing the proof size and CRS size of NIZK, a very efficient family of NIZK proof system is developed, known as zk-SNARKs. Zk-SNARKs can generate a succinct proof that verifiers with less computing power can also effectively verify proofs quickly and zk-SNARKs based on the CRS model became quite popular.

A zk-SNARK protocol based on CRS is described by three algorithms that work as follows:

- *Gen* is the setup algorithm, generating a necessary string *crs* used later in the proving process and some verification key *vrs*, sometimes assumed to be secret to the verifier only. A trusted party typically runs it.
- *Prove* is the proving algorithm that inputs the *crs*, the statement *u* and a corresponding witness *w* and outputs the proof π.
- *Verify* is the algorithm that takes as input the verification key *vrs*, the statement *u* and the proof π, and returns 1 to accept the proof or 0 to reject"

In 2010, Jens Groth et al. [19] proposed the Knowledge of Exponent Assumption (KEA). By adopting this controversial assumption, Groth reduced the length of zero-knowledge proofs based on pairing to a constant level with the cost of CRS size by hiding some secret random values in the CRS. This solution took a big step forward in the practical development of zero-knowledge proof but also brought a technical problem, which became a focus of attention in the application of the blockchain field, which is the Trusted-Setup. In any case, this scheme greatly promoted the development of zk-SNARKs.

In 2012, Bitansky et al. [30] formally introduced the acronym zk-SNARK. At this time, it was generally realized that only the proof length of zk-SNARKs must be small enough; the practicality of zk-SNARKs would be stronger. In the same year, Lipmaa [25] improved Groth's zk-SNARK [19] by reducing the length of CRS and the computational complexity of the prover by using a (presumably) weaker security assumption. The prover's computational complexity was reduced to a quasilinear size in this paper.

In 2013, based on Groth's 2010 work [19], continuing with the idea of verifying polynomial equations, Gennaro [21] introduced the technology of the Quadratic Span Program (QSP) and Quadratic Arithmetic Program (QAP). In their paper, Gennaro reduced the circuit satisfiability problem to a statement about QSPs through circuit coding and Lagrange interpolation and presented a zk-SNARK where CRS length is proportional to statement and witness size. Gennaro's work significantly shortened the proof time and compressed the proof length to a small constant level, which was much more efficient. Subsequently, in the same year, Parno et al. [26] optimized and improved based on Gennaro's work and implemented a verifiable computing protocol called Pinocchio, where verification was less than ten milliseconds, calculations were less than 300 bytes, and the proof time was close to linear.

Lipmma [31] proposed a more efficient QSP combined with error correction codes. Danezis et al. [32] redefine quadratic span programs as square span programs and gave a program for boolean circuits containing 4 group elements. Bitansky et al. [33] presented an abstract model of SNARKs based on the linear encoding of domain elements, LIPs (Linear-interactive Proofs), which captures the feature that the prover is limited to only using linear operations to compute messages. In addition, this paper presents a general transformation—from 2 rounds of LIP combined with pairing-based techniques to publicly verifiable SNARKs or combined with homomorphic encryption to obtain SNARKs for designated verifiers.

In 2016, Groth et al. [28] improved the Pinocchio protocol [26], strengthening the security assumptions and compressing the proof size and verification complexity. In Groth's protocol, the proof only had 3 group elements, which became the most widely used zero-knowledge proof technology solution in the blockchain field and one of the most efficient zk-SNARK until today.

We compared different zk-SNARK protocols based on CRS in terms of CRS size, the complexity of communication, proof, and verification, and the comparison results are as follows:

Table 1. Comparison of zk-SNARKs based on CRS from different perspectives

Article	CRS size	Communication	Prover	Verifier
[19]	$O(\lvert C \rvert^2)$	$42G$	$\Theta(\lvert C \rvert^2)$	$\Theta(\lvert C \rvert)M$ $\Theta(\lvert 1 \rvert)P$
[21]	$O(\lvert C \rvert)$	$9G$	$O(\lvert C \rvert \log \lvert C \rvert)$ $O(\lvert C \rvert)$	$O(\lvert io \rvert)E$ $14P$
[26]	$O(\lvert C \rvert)$	$8G$	$O(\lvert C \rvert \log \lvert C \rvert)$ $O(\lvert C \rvert)$	$O(\lvert io \rvert)E$ $11P$
[28]	$O(\lvert C \rvert)$	$2G_1, 1G_2$	$O(\lvert C \rvert)$	$O(\lvert io \rvert)E$ $4P$

In Table 1, G is a group element, E is a group power operation, P is a pairwise operation on a bilinear group, M is the number of multiplication gates in the circuit, $O(\lvert io \rvert)$ is preprocessing overhead of zk-SNARKs based on QAP.

Although zero-knowledge proofs have evolved to achieve very good results in terms of proof size, proof complexity, and verification complexity, traditional CRS-based zk-SNARKs still suffer from two shortcomings: one is that most zk-SNARKs can only target specific circuits. Different circuits need to generate different CRSs, and one is that the generation of CRSs inevitably requires the inclusion of trusted third parties. And one is that the generation of CRSs inevitably requires the inclusion of trusted third parties.

4   Universal Updatable zk-SNARK

Zk-SNARKs based on the CRS model had shortcomings in generality because CRS could often only target specific circuits, not arbitrary circuits. In order to solve this problem, people started to study universal updatable zk-SNARK.

In order to replace the CRS model, Groth et al. [34] defined the Updatable Model, a compromise model between the complete CRS model and the complete Bare Public Key model. Under this model, the participating parties can arbitrarily update the CRS. Update interactively, and this update is verifiable. As long as at least one of all parties involved is honest, the simulated trapdoor will not be leaked, thus replacing trusted third parties. In addition, such updatable CRSs are universal; that is to say, their generation does not depend on specific circuits, so that they can be used for zero-knowledge proofs of arbitrary circuits.

In 2019, Maller et al. presented an efficient, general, and updatable SNARK called Sonic [35], whose proof length was an endless number of group elements, and the CRS scale was only linear in the circuit size. The technical goal of Sonic is to make a zero-knowledge argument for the satisfiability of a constraint system representing an NP-hard language, which is similar to the constraint system in Bulletproofs [70] and is also expressed as a bivariate polynomial equation.

Plonk [75] is an improvement on Snoic. Plonk protocol is centred on proving consistency between circuit gates using permutation checks, which improves the proof time but simplifies the permutation argument and arithmetic process.

Then, Setty decided to apply polynomial commitment to achieve improvements in verification complexity without trust settings, and a zk-SNARK called Spartan [61] has been designed where the prover complexity is $O(|C|\log|C|)$ while both the proof length and the verifier complexity are $O(\log^2|C|)$.

In 2020, Chiesa et al. [37] also improved the Sonic protocol. They presented the Marlin protocol, which had a CRS length linear to the circuit scale and a proof length of an endless number of group elements, and both were shorter than Sonic. Marlin had a very short proof time and verification time. The core of Marlin's technology is an efficient Algebraic Holographic Proof against R1CS (Rank-1 Constraint Satisfiability), which can be implemented under linear proof length and constant query complexity.

In the same year, Ben Fisch et al. [71] published their latest breakthrough in zero-knowledge proofs, dubbed "Supersonic". Supersonic is a breakthrough in cryptography and zero-knowledge proofs, which introduces a new, efficient polynomial commitment scheme for existing polynomial IOPs, called Diophantine Arguments of Knowledge.

Campanelli et al. [76] proposed a new solution in 2021: Lunar. Lunar sacrifices the verification part, including verification time and verification key length, but achieves a better proof length and proof time. It also proposes a new algebraic IOP and a new cryptographic compiler to construct a generic zk-SNARK.

We compared the complexity of different universal updatable zk-SNARK protocols in terms of communication, proof, verification, and preprocessing. The comparison results are as follows:

Table 2. Comparison of universal updatable zk-SNARKs

Protocol	Pre.	Com.	Prover	Verifier
Snoic [35]	$O(|C|\log|C|)$	$O(1)$	$O(|C|\log|C|)$	$O(N + \log|C|)$
Spartan [61]	$O(|C|)$	$O(\log^2|C|)$	$O(|C|\log|C|)$	$O(\log^2|C|)$
Marlin [37]	$O(|C|\log|C|)$	$O(|C|)$	$O(|C|\log|C|)$	$O(N + \log|C|)$
Supersnoic [71]	$O(|C|\log|C|)$	$O(\log|C|)$	$O(|C|\log|C|)$	$O(\log|C|)$

In Table 2, N is the length of the inputs and outputs of the computation.

5 Transparent zk-SNARK

Trusted third parties are essential for zk-SNARKs based on the traditional CRS model. This shortcoming, however, is intolerable for decentralized systems such as blockchain. So is a trusted third party a must for zk-SNARKs? With the gradual deepening of zero-knowledge proofs, researchers have proposed the concept of transparent zero-knowledge proofs. Moreover, in such transparent zk-SNARKs, the generation of CRS does not require the presence of trusted third parties, which precisely meets the needs of decentralized systems and fits better with applications such as blockchain.

Although researchers at a relatively early stage proposed making zk-SNARKs transparent, there was still a long interval before the first practical and transparent zk-SNARK protocol was created. Until Ben-Sasson et al. [38] wrote the first papers describing transparent zk-SNARK, the concept of Zero-knowledge Scalable Transparent Argument of Knowledge (zk-STARK) was formally introduced. In 2018, Ben-Sasson et al. [38] first proposed the STARK scheme. In STARK, it is first necessary to convert the circuit to be proved into an Algebraic Intermediate Representation which represents a circuit's execution as transitions of the circuit's intermediate states (including input and output states). In this way, the circuit can be represented by these transitions of adjacent states. Then Algebraic Placement and Routing technology was used to optimize the constraints of the circuit, and the satisfiability of the circuit was transformed into two groups of Reed-Solomon Proximity Testing Problem, which could be solved by using the Fast Reed-Solomon Validity IOP protocol. To summarize, STARK uses publicly verifiable randomness to create untrustworthy computational systems.

In the same year, Wahby et al. [39] proposed the Hyrax, based on the optimized Giraffe interactive proof protocol, which has low communication and cost for the prover and verifier. In Hyrax, Wahby used two approaches to make it more efficient; one is to optimize the IP structure by combining verification algorithms, multiple commitment schemes and Schnorr [40] based proofs; the other is to propose a new proof commitment scheme, which reduces the computation time of the verifier.

Ben-Sasson et al. [41] proposed a zk-STARK for R1CS instances called Aurora. Aurora implements efficient checking of R1CS instances by proposing the protocol called Sumcheck to prevent its performance from receiving the effects of the R1CS structure.

Based on recursive proof techniques for discrete logarithmic problems and optimal inner product valuation, Bünz et al. [70] designed a novel non-interactive ZKP model called Bulletproofs. The most important feature of the Bulletproofs protocol is that the size of the proofs it produces is logarithmically transformed. Also, Bulletproofs is an excellent zero-knowledge range proof. In this model, the size of the range proofs is linear, a property that makes it more suitable for distributed scenarios such as blockchains.

The Fractal proposed by Chiesa et al. [42] in 2019 is a zk-STARK for R1CS statement. The scheme constructs a new holographic proof for R1CS assertion. It provides a transformation method from holographic IOP to transparent preprocessed SNARK, thus realizing the construction of transparent preprocessed SNARK for R1CS class.

In addition, the transparent zk-SNARK is usually based on Random Oracle Model (ROM). ROM is an idealized cryptographic model that assumes the existence of a truly random function such that all parties involved in the protocol have access to this function.

In reality, however, no such assumed completely random ideal function exists. So the researchers heuristically assumed that a sufficiently good hash function is a random oracle.

We compared the complexity of different transparent zk-SNARK protocols in terms of communication, proof, verification and preprocessing. The comparison results are as follows (Table 3):

Table 3. Comparison of transparent zk-SNARKs

Protocol	Pre.	Com.	Prover	Verifier
STARK [35]	No	$O(\log^2|C|)$	$O(|C|\log^2|C|)$	$O(|C|)$
Bulletproofs [70]	$O(1)$	$O(\log M)$	$O(M)$	$O(M)$
Aurora [41]	No	$O(\log^2|C|)$	$O(|C|\log|C|)$	$O(|C|)$
Fractal [42]	$O(|C|\log|C|)$	$O(|C|)$	$O(|C|\log|C|)$	$O(N + \log|C|)$

In Table 2, N is the length of the inputs and outputs of the computation, M is the number of multiplication gates in the circuit.

6 MPC-in-the-Head

The MPC [77] technique enables multiple parties who do not trust each other to collaboratively compute any function and output the result of the computation, with the guarantee that no party can obtain any information other than the result of the computation to which it is entitled. This property allows zero-knowledge proofs to be closely related to the existence of MPC (Fig. 1).

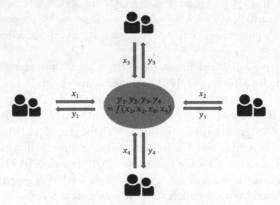

Fig. 1. Secure multi-party computation

In 2007, Ishai et al. [98] first introduced the concept of MPC-in-the-head (MPCith), which means that the prover first executes the MPC protocol "in the head" and then commits to the copy seen by each participant "in the head" and sends it to the verifier. Then the verifier V interacts with P to determine whether to believe P's assertion. The advantages of constructing zk-SNARK based on MPCith are that it does not require a trustworthy setup, the proof time is efficient, and it is resistant to quantum attacks. Based on this, Giacomelli et al. [68] published the ZKBoo scheme, which eliminates the interactions compared to the scheme [67], and the proof time is almost 1000 times faster than the previous zk-SNARKs, with the disadvantage that the communication complexity is linear in the circuit size. Chase et al. improved the scheme [68] by reducing the proof length by more than half without increasing the computational cost. Succinct zero-knowledge proof protocols based on MPCith also include ZKB++ [78], KKW18 [79], and Ligero [85], which are compared as shown as follows:

Table 4. Zero-Knowledge proofs based on MPC

Protocol	MPC protocol	Com.	Prover	Verifier
ZKBoo [68]	GMW [36]	$O(|C|)$	$O(|C|)$	$O(M)$
ZKB++ [78]	GMW	$O(|C|)$	$O(|C|)$	$O(M)$
KKW18 [79]	[69]	$O(|C|+n\lambda_s)$	$O(|C|)$	$O(|C|)$
Ligero [53]	No	$O(\sqrt{|C|})$	$O(|C|\log|C|)$	$O(|C|\log|C|)$

In Table 4, M is the number of multiplication gates in the circuit, n is the number of participants, λ_s is seed length of the pseudo-random generator.

Each party using MPCith can perform distributed computing based on its input, and each party generates a script. Although MPCith divides the secret into multiple parties, they need to work together to use it; if only part of the shared secret is disclosed, the secret is still unknown. MPCith is efficient for boolean circuits and is extensible, but unfortunately, it is unsuitable for scenarios requiring on-chain verification.

7 Applications in Blockchain

In the context of the globalization of the digital economy, the emergence of the blockchain has technically solved the security problems brought about by the trust-based centralized model for the first time. However, the openness and transparency of the blockchain have also brought great challenges to people's privacy protection. Two important features of zero-knowledge proof technology are the main factors that make it applicable in the blockchain field: 1) Zero-knowledge proof can protect the privacy of data and prove it without leaking data; 2) Zero-knowledge proofs only need to generate proofs with a small amount of data to complete proofs for large batches of data. This chapter will introduce the direction of the combination of zero-knowledge proof and blockchain, as well as specific application cases.

7.1 Privacy Protection

Asset information is important in a person's or an organization's private information. The exposure of account asset information and insider information about asset transactions to the public is undoubtedly a huge risk and threat to asset management. One of the main features of blockchain is the public ledger, where all transaction information can be tracked publicly. Although this solves the problem of information asymmetry and fraud to a certain extent, it does pose a great danger to the privacy of account assets. Once a user is associated with a wallet address on the blockchain, all of the user's asset information and transaction information will be exposed.

As a peer-to-peer public ledger, once all data on the blockchain is made public, people will inevitably be concerned about their private data, such as personally identifiable information and asset information. For this reason, blockchain practitioners have proposed several solutions to this problem. Such as replacing a new address, cryptocurrency hybrid technology, ring symbols, and zero-knowledge proofs. Among them, the advantages of zero-knowledge proof are the most obvious. Zero-knowledge proof as a technical tool aims to guarantee the correctness of data while protecting its privacy. It can complete a transaction by submitting proof without information leakage. It achieves complete anonymity of transaction information and can support large-scale transactions, and it is therefore adopted to achieve privacy protection of transactions and assets on the blockchain.

7.2 Expansion

With the increasing understanding and recognition of the public, more and more blockchain-based technology applications have been explored. However, the blockchain's performance has made it difficult to meet the current needs. On the one hand, due to the constraints of decentralized network data transmission and node synchronization, the block size is very limited, so the number of transactions that each block can accommodate is very limited, and the data that the blockchain can store is also very limited; On the one hand, due to the existence of the block synchronization mechanism, transactions cannot be processed in time, which seriously hinders the migration of traditional application scenarios that have extremely high requirements on response speed to the blockchain.

Zero-knowledge proofs only need to generate a small amount of data to complete the proofs of large batches of data. Many technical experts have noticed the potential of this feature of zero-knowledge proofs for solving blockchain performance bottlenecks early on. Vitalik, the founder of Ethereum, said that by using zk-SNARK to verify transactions on a large scale, the scale of asset transactions could be expanded on Ethereum. With zk-SNARKs, 500 transactions per second can be processed on Ethereum. That was more than 30 times the number of transactions per second that the Ethereum network could handle at the time. Currently, many expansion solutions are based on zero-knowledge proof, mainly in three directions: off-chain expansion, on-chain block compression and lightweight client.

Off-Chain Capacity Expansion

Off-chain scaling refers to establishing a layered structure of peripheral or second-layer transaction networks outside the main chain of cryptocurrencies, transferring most of the calculations to off-chain or side chains to complete. In contrast, the main chain only submits a very small amount—the result of calculating the amount of data. So far, there have been many attempts by technical experts in the expansion of blockchain, and some more mature layered solutions have been put into use.

One of the core problems in implementing the layered scheme is ensuring the authenticity of the data submitted from the Layer-2 network to the main chain. Zero-knowledge proof is an important solution to this problem. First of all, the important feature of zero-knowledge proof - it only needs to generate proof of a small amount of data to complete the proof of a large amount of data, which is very suitable for the layered scheme to complete the data calculation in the second layer and only submit a large amount of data to the main chain. Second, the mathematical characteristics of zero-knowledge proof ensure that as long as the data submitted to the main chain can pass the verification, the data is correct, and the calculation completed by the second-layer network is credible. Therefore, the zero-knowledge proof technology achieves higher concurrency without sacrificing the security of the original blockchain. As the data submitted to the blockchain has become more concise, the cost of completing transactions and executing contracts has also been greatly reduced.

The zk-Rollup scheme is a secondary expansion scheme based on zero-knowledge proof. Each state transition needs to provide zero-knowledge proof, verified by the contract on the main chain. The state can only be changed after the verification passes; each state transition strictly relies on cryptographic proof. Compared with the similar scheme Optimistic Rollup, ZK Rollup has overwhelming advantages in terms of security.

It is estimated that zk-Rollup could increase Ethereum's throughput to approximately 3000 transactions per second (fps) after the completion of the Istanbul upgrade. Many expansion solutions and applications are based on zk-Rollup, such as ZKSync and Loopring 3.0 protocol (Fig. 2).

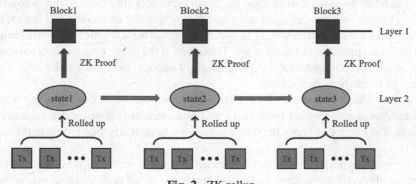

Fig. 2. ZK rollup

On-Chain Block Compression

On the blockchain, the size of a block is limited, and the number of transactions that each block can hold is also limited. Therefore, if the amount of data per transaction can be reduced, the number of transactions a block can carry is also limited. Will increase. Therefore, in addition to expanding off-chain, block data compression is also an important idea to improve the throughput of the blockchain.

The compression implemented by using zero-knowledge proof also provides many benefits for the application on the chain: On the one hand, it solves the problem that the amount of data processed in many practical businesses is very large and cannot be put on the chain at all. On the other hand, the cost is reduced. After the compressed data is submitted to the chain, the handling fee will also decrease. Therefore, block compression technology increases the possibility of more applications on the chain.

Similar to off-chain extensions, the key to implementing block compression is verifying the compressed data's authenticity. Again, zero-knowledge proofs can still play a big role here. With zero-knowledge proofs, there is no need to submit the complete data to the chain to ensure the correct execution of the business. As a result, many business processes under the chain can be compressed into small proof. The smart contract can then validate the submitted proof to ensure there is no possibility of cheating by the service node. This way, many calculations that would otherwise run slowly and expensively are shifted off-chain. Only a small amount of data is needed on-chain for proofs to replace the many business processes that would otherwise be performed.

Lightweight Client

With the continuous accumulation of blocks and the growth of the business, the data volume of the full node is also increasing, so the full node of the blockchain will become huge, making network synchronization and storage difficult. Because on the one hand, it takes a long time to download hundreds of gigabytes or even several terabytes of full-node data; on the other hand, full-nodes need to fully verify the downloaded data to ensure the correctness of the data. In most blockchains. In the verification process, all transactions of the full node need to be executed in sequence and compared with the downloaded status. Each full node must be verified once, which is very time-consuming. Subject to the requirements of hardware equipment and the complexity of running full nodes, it is very difficult for most ordinary users to synchronize full nodes, which seriously hinders the large-scale application of blockchain. Therefore, if the above problems are solved by technical means, the construction of a lightweight client is essential for the large-scale business of blockchain applications.

SNARK schemes can be used for delegating computation in the following way: a server can run a computation for a client and non-interactively prove the accuracy of the result. The client can verify the result's correctness in nearly-linear time in the input size.

The compression power of zero-knowledge proofs comes into play again. At the same time, the verification ability of zero-knowledge proof is used. However, without sacrificing security, it can solve the problem that each full node must repeatedly verify the transaction block data during block synchronization. So zero-knowledge proofs provide a good solution for building lightweight clients.

7.3 Applications

In blockchain-based applications, zero-knowledge proofs are often used to solve data privacy issues and blockchain expansion. The solution based on zero-knowledge proof provides reliable mathematical proof rather than trust based on a third party, helping to achieve fair exchanges of goods, services and data. For example, using zero-knowledge contingent payments for services [70]. Zero-knowledge arguments have also been used to prove the solvency of cryptocurrency exchanges [71] and blockchain applications involving Internet of Things (IoT) devices [13] and electronic voting [72]. In traditional blockchain applications, transaction data must be publicly verifiable for consensus algorithms to work. Therefore, solutions based on zero-knowledge proof must protect sensitive data while maintaining public verifiability. This section will analyze the specific use cases of zero-knowledge proof in the blockchain.

There is a flaw in Bitcoin transactions: in the transaction process of Bitcoin, the transferor's address and the transfer receiver's address can be linked. Through transaction data mining and tracking user information on Bitcoin, the "identity" on Bitcoin can even be linked to the real identity. Zerocoin [58] is a solution to this problem. In the transaction process of Zerocoin, there is a Zerocoin Mint step. You need to convert a certain amount of Bitcoin into Zerocoin and then convert Zerocoin into Bitcoin when you transfer money. Zerocoin uses zero-knowledge proof in casting zero coins and redeeming zero coins to hide the sender and receiver information corresponding to a transaction. The protocol uses a zero-knowledge argument based on the Schnorr signature [59] and is non-interactive, utilizing the Fiat-Shamir heuristic. Nevertheless, the proof is large, and verification is slow.

Zerocash [60] can be considered an improved version of Zerocoin. It is based on zk-SNARKs to implement a decentralized anonymous payment (DAP) scheme. Compared to Zerocoin, Zerocash has a much-reduced proof length and verification time, but a common reference string must be generated beforehand. In addition, Zerocash hides both sides of the transaction and the amount of the transaction. The Zerocash protocol was eventually used in the Zcash cryptocurrency. One of the biggest problems related to decentralized currencies is their use for illegal activities such as extortion and money laundering [62].

Filecoin is a distributed storage project based on the Interplanetary File System (IPFS). When saving files, Filecoin builds a Merkle tree of the original data, performs hash calculation layer by layer, and uploads the value of the tree root to the blockchain chain. After the data is linked, Filecoin needs to verify the data on a randomly selected Merkle leaf node every other period and calculate all the paths from the root to the leaf. This process uses storage-proof technology based on zero-knowledge proof. If the node required to provide proof does not store the corresponding data, it cannot provide the hash values of all the critical paths in a limited time and thus cannot pass the verification. In this way, we verify the validity of data storage through zero-knowledge proof without exposing the stored data itself.

· CryptoNote is a protocol for implementing untraceable and unlinkable cryptocurrencies using anonymity sets. It applies the ring signature originally proposed by Rivest et al. [49] to hide the identity of the payer and the payee's identity and the amount. Monero [51], a cryptocurrency originally based on CryptoNote, uses a combination of three mechanisms-hidden addresses, ring signatures to achieve privacy protection for transaction data. Later, due to attacks on the linkability of transactions [52], Monero turned to a rather robust zero-knowledge argument using Bulletproofs scheme [70].

Quisquis [63] improves on Monero using updatable public keys. In both Monero and Zerocash, the size of the Unspent Transaction Output (UTXO) set increases due to the ambiguity of the transaction addresses. Quisquis attempts to eliminate this drawback by allowing users to create their own anonymous sets for private transactions. Privacy is ensured through updatable public keys and zero-knowledge arguments to show that the keys have been updated and the assets have not been stolen.

Solidus [67] is a protocol for confidential transactions on a public blockchain that follows the account model. In contrast to contemporary cryptocurrencies, user accounts are maintained by banks, which mediate the hidden amounts and transactions of the parties. However, each transaction can be publicly verified on the blockchain using a zero-knowledge argument. Regulation is possible due to the presence of banks, but auditing requires opening the transactions and cannot be done publicly.

PGC [68] is an auditable decentralized confidential trading system. As an innovative confidential transaction solution, the PGC team introduced the concept of distributed confidential transaction system (DCP) with audibility to balance privacy and auditability. PGC guarantees the privacy of transactions and supports the audit of privacy protection. On the one hand, PGC realizes the privacy protection of transaction data sources by using integrated signature and encryption schemes; on the other hand, it uses non-interactive zero-knowledge argumentation to enable users to prove their compliance.

Zether [64] is the first smart contract scheme based on the account model in Ethereum. It uses zero knowledge proof to conceal the transaction amount and the addresses of both parties. However, Zether still faces problems such as high gas fees and possible exposure of account addresses when paying gas fees.

ZoKrates is a zk-SNARKs tool project for Ethereum. It can be used to generate zero-knowledge proofs under the chain easily and then submit them to the Ethereum chain for verification with smart contracts. EYBlockchain provides a relatively complete privacy transaction service on Ethereum based on ZoKrates using smart contracts on Ethereum.

Aztec is a privacy and capacity expansion solution based on ZK Rollup. It accesses privacy through a zero-knowledge proof system called Plonk [75]. All transactions within Aztec are private, and parties other than Aztec cannot view internal activities. Based on Aztec, zk.money is a shielding protocol and a portal for users to access Aztec from the Ethereum main network.

ZkSync is one of the most popular Layer-2 solutions. ZkSync introduces two roles of validators and guardians to improve the scalability of the blockchain. The verifier is responsible for processing the transaction, packaging the block, and providing zero-knowledge proof for the transaction to prove that the transaction process is correct. The protector is responsible for nominating the verifier of the next block and monitoring whether the block is processed correctly. At present, Ethereum Virtual Machine based on zero-knowledge proof is one of the research objectives of zkSync.

8 Trends and Outlook

The zero-knowledge proof theory is in an extremely important basic position in cryptography. In terms of application, the strong privacy protection feature of zero-knowledge proof makes it widely used in identity authentication, group signature, secure multi-party computing, cryptocurrency, electronic voting and other fields. This article analyses the development process of different zero-knowledge proof technologies and their applications, from interactive zero-knowledge proof to NIZK proofs to zk-SNARKs to zero-knowledge proof protocols without a trusted setup. Comparing their development process, we can see that zero-knowledge proofs have been developing in the direction of succinctness, decentralization, and universality. Current zero-knowledge proofs have done well in terms of functionality, simplicity, and efficiency, but there is still much room for improvement. For this reason, we have listed the following possible future trends:

- Further improve the efficiency of non-interactive zero-knowledge proofs and reduce the complexity of communication, proof, and verification.
- Explore more ways to build generic updatable zk-SNARKs.
- Make further efficiency optimizations for transparent zero-knowledge proof protocols for zk-SNARKs.
- Select or design more suitable MPC protocols for zk-SNARKs that simulate secure multi-party computation.
- Optimize the underlying cryptographic editor to reduce the practical application overhead.
- Explore how to improve further the security of zero-knowledge proofs and further integration with decentralized system applications such as blockchain.

Currently, zero-knowledge proof has rich application scenarios in the blockchain field, and has been proven to be an effective solution to the problems of blockchain privacy and capacity expansion. However, we believe that the potential of zero-knowledge proof goes beyond this. We believe it is currently in the early stage of a series of development of the zero-knowledge proof scheme, but there is no doubt that the blockchain will become an important platform for zero-knowledge proof. The confidentiality and scalability of zero-knowledge proof will provide a new direction for the development of decentralization. On the one hand, we can foresee that with the growing demand of users for privacy security, zero-knowledge proofs will become an effective tool to help users control their data and selectively share personal information. On the other hand, zero-knowledge proofs will greatly improve the performance of the blockchain and help more users to participate in blockchain activities more easily and comfortably, thus promoting the development of decentralization which will greatly expand a series of new possibilities of Web3.

9 Conclusion

In this paper, we give a clear overview of the development of zero-knowledge proofs and compare different zero-knowledge proof protocols in terms of communication complexity, proof size and proof time. We also study the blockchain environment's zero-knowledge proof protocols and the combined application of zero-knowledge proofs and blockchain. Finally, we summarize the development direction of zero-knowledge and give an outlook on its future development trends.

Acknowledgements. This work was financially supported by the Key-Area Research and Development Program of Guangdong Province (No. 2020B1111370001), National Key R&D Program of China (No. 2018YFB1800705) and National Natural Science Foundation of China (No. 82271267).

References

1. Goldwasser, S., Micali, S., Rackoff, C.: The knowledge complexity of interactive proof systems. SIAM J. Comput. **18**(1), 186–208 (1989)
2. Blum, M., Feldman, P., Micali, S.: Non-interactive zero-knowledge and its applications. In: Providing Sound Foundations for Cryptography: On the Work of Shafi Goldwasser and Silvio Micali, pp. 329–349 (2019)
3. Brassard, G., Crepeau, C.: Non-transitive transfer of confidence: a perfect zero-knowledge interactive protocol for SAT and beyond. In: 27th Annual Symposium on Foundations of Computer Science, SFCS 1986, pp. 188–195. IEEE (1986)
4. Goldwasser, S., Micali, S., Rivest, R.L.: A "Paradoxical" solution to the signature problem. In: 25th Annual Symposium on Foundations of Computer Science, pp. 441–448 (1984). https://doi.org/10.1109/SFCS.1984.715946
5. Boyar, J., Brassard, G., Peralta, R.: Subquadratic zero-knowledge. J. ACM (JACM) **42**(6), 1169–1193 (1995)
6. Kilian, J.: A note on efficient zero-knowledge proofs and arguments. In: Proceedings of the Twenty-Fourth Annual ACM Symposium on Theory of Computing, pp. 723–732 (1992)
7. Cramer, R., Damgård, I.: Zero-knowledge proofs for finite field arithmetic, or: can zero-knowledge be for free. In: Krawczyk, H. (ed.) CRYPTO 1998. LNCS, vol. 1462, pp. 424–441. Springer, Heidelberg (1998). https://doi.org/10.1007/BFb0055745
8. Fiat, A., Shamir, A.: How to prove yourself: practical solutions to identification and signature problems. In: Odlyzko, A.M. (ed.) CRYPTO 1986. LNCS, vol. 263, pp. 186–194. Springer, Heidelberg (1987). https://doi.org/10.1007/3-540-47721-7_12
9. De Santis, A., Di Crescenzo, G., Persiano, G.: The knowledge complexity of quadratic residuosity languages. Theoret. Comput. Sci. **132**(1–2), 291–317 (1994)
10. Feige, U., Lapidot, D., Shamir, A.: Multiple non-interactive zero knowledge proofs random-string. In: Proceedings of the 31st Annual Symposium on Foundations of Computer Science, pp. 308–317
11. Blum, M., De Santis, A., Micali, S., et al.: Noninteractive zero-knowledge. SIAM J. Comput. **20**(6), 1084–1118 (1991)
12. Lapidot, D., Shamir, A.: Publicly verifiable non-interactive zero-knowledge proofs. In: Menezes, A.J., Vanstone, S.A. (eds.) CRYPTO 1990. LNCS, vol. 537, pp. 353–365. Springer, Heidelberg (1991). https://doi.org/10.1007/3-540-38424-3_26
13. Damgård, I.: Non-interactive circuit based proofs and non-interactive perfect zero-knowledge with preprocessing. In: Rueppel, R.A. (ed.) EUROCRYPT 1992. LNCS, vol. 658, pp. 341–355. Springer, Heidelberg (1993). https://doi.org/10.1007/3-540-47555-9_28
14. Kilian, J.: On the complexity of bounded-interaction and noninteractive zero-knowledge proofs. In: Proceedings 35th Annual Symposium on Foundations of Computer Science, pp. 466–477. IEEE (1994)

15. De Santis, A., Persiano, G., Di Crescenzo, G.: Non-interactive zero-knowledge: a low-randomness characterization of NP (extended abstract). In: Wiedermann, J., van Emde Boas, P., Nielsen, M. (eds.) ICALP 1999. LNCS, vol. 1644, pp. 271–280. Springer, Heidelberg (1999). https://doi.org/10.1007/3-540-48523-6_24

16. Boyar, J., Damgård, I., Peralta, R.: Short non-interactive cryptographic proofs. J. Cryptol. **13**(4), 449–472 (2000)

17. Groth, J., Ostrovsky, R., Sahai, A.: Non-interactive zaps and new techniques for NIZK. In: Dwork, C. (ed.) CRYPTO 2006. LNCS, vol. 4117, pp. 97–111. Springer, Heidelberg (2006). https://doi.org/10.1007/11818175_6

18. Groth, J., Ostrovsky, R., Sahai, A.: New techniques for noninteractive zero-knowledge. J. ACM (JACM) **59**(3), 1–35 (2012)

19. Groth, J.: Short pairing-based non-interactive zero-knowledge arguments. In: Abe, M. (ed.) ASIACRYPT 2010. LNCS, vol. 6477, pp. 321–340. Springer, Heidelberg (2010). https://doi.org/10.1007/978-3-642-17373-8_19

20. De Santis, A., Micali, S., Persiano, G.: Non-interactive zero-knowledge with preprocessing. In: Goldwasser, S. (ed.) CRYPTO 1988. LNCS, vol. 403, pp. 269–282. Springer, New York (1990). https://doi.org/10.1007/0-387-34799-2_21

21. Gennaro, R., Gentry, C., Parno, B., Raykova, M.: Quadratic span programs and succinct NIZKs without PCPs. In: Johansson, T., Nguyen, P.Q. (eds.) EUROCRYPT 2013. LNCS, vol. 7881, pp. 626–645. Springer, Heidelberg (2013). https://doi.org/10.1007/978-3-642-38348-9_37

22. Babai, L., Fortnow, L., Levin, L.A., et al.: Checking computations in polylogarithmic time. In: Proceedings of the Twenty-Third Annual ACM Symposium on Theory of Computing, pp. 21–32 (1991)

23. Feige, U., Goldwasser, S., Lovász, L., et al.: Interactive proofs and the hardness of approximating cliques. J. ACM (JACM) **43**(2), 268–292 (1996)

24. Arora, S., Lund, C., Motwani, R., et al.: Proof verification and the hardness of approximation problems. J. ACM (JACM) **45**(3), 501–555 (1998)

25. Lipmaa, H.: Progression-free sets and sublinear pairing-based non-interactive zero-knowledge arguments. In: Cramer, R. (ed.) TCC 2012. LNCS, vol. 7194, pp. 169–189. Springer, Heidelberg (2012). https://doi.org/10.1007/978-3-642-28914-9_10

26. Parno, B., Howell, J., Gentry, C., et al.: Pinocchio: nearly practical verifiable computation. In: 2013 IEEE Symposium on Security and Privacy, pp. 238–252. IEEE (2013)

27. Bitansky, N., Canetti, R., Chiesa, A., et al.: Recursive composition and bootstrapping for SNARKs and proof-carrying data. In: Proceedings of the Forty-Fifth Annual ACM Symposium on Theory of Computing, pp. 111–120 (2013)

28. Groth, J.: On the size of pairing-based non-interactive arguments. In: Fischlin, M., Coron, J.-S. (eds.) EUROCRYPT 2016. LNCS, vol. 9666, pp. 305–326. Springer, Heidelberg (2016). https://doi.org/10.1007/978-3-662-49896-5_11

29. Groth, J., Maller, M.: Snarky signatures: minimal signatures of knowledge from simulation-extractable SNARKs. In: Katz, J., Shacham, H. (eds.) CRYPTO 2017. LNCS, vol. 10402, pp. 581–612. Springer, Cham (2017). https://doi.org/10.1007/978-3-319-63715-0_20

30. Bitansky, N., et al.: Why "Fiat-Shamir for proofs" lacks a proof. In: Sahai, A. (ed.) TCC 2013. LNCS, vol. 7785, pp. 182–201. Springer, Heidelberg (2013). https://doi.org/10.1007/978-3-642-36594-2_11

31. Lipmaa, H.: Succinct non-interactive zero knowledge arguments from span programs and linear error-correcting codes. In: Sako, K., Sarkar, P. (eds.) ASIACRYPT 2013. LNCS, vol. 8269, pp. 41–60. Springer, Heidelberg (2013). https://doi.org/10.1007/978-3-642-42033-7_3

32. Danezis, G., Fournet, C., Groth, J., Kohlweiss, M.: Square span programs with applications to succinct NIZK arguments. In: Sarkar, P., Iwata, T. (eds.) ASIACRYPT 2014. LNCS, vol.

8873, pp. 532–550. Springer, Heidelberg (2014). https://doi.org/10.1007/978-3-662-45611-8_28

33. Bitansky, N., Chiesa, A., Ishai, Y., Paneth, O., Ostrovsky, R.: Succinct non-interactive arguments via linear interactive proofs. In: Sahai, A. (ed.) TCC 2013. LNCS, vol. 7785, pp. 315–333. Springer, Heidelberg (2013). https://doi.org/10.1007/978-3-642-36594-2_18

34. Groth, J., Kohlweiss, M., Maller, M., Meiklejohn, S., Miers, I.: Updatable and universal common reference strings with applications to zk-SNARKs. In: Shacham, H., Boldyreva, A. (eds.) CRYPTO 2018. LNCS, vol. 10993, pp. 698–728. Springer, Cham (2018). https://doi.org/10.1007/978-3-319-96878-0_24

35. Maller, M., Bowe, S., Kohlweiss, M., et al.: Sonic: zero-knowledge SNARKs from linear-size universal and updatable structured reference strings. In: Proceedings of the 2019 ACM SIGSAC Conference on Computer and Communications Security, pp. 2111–2128 (2019)

36. Goldreich, O., Micali, S., Wigderson, A.: How to play any mental game, or a completeness theorem for protocols with honest majority. In: Providing Sound Foundations for Cryptography: On the Work of Shafi Goldwasser and Silvio Micali, pp. 307–328 (2019)

37. Chiesa, A., Hu, Y., Maller, M., Mishra, P., Vesely, N., Ward, N.: Marlin: preprocessing zkSNARKs with universal and updatable SRS. In: Canteaut, A., Ishai, Y. (eds.) EUROCRYPT 2020. LNCS, vol. 12105, pp. 738–768. Springer, Cham (2020). https://doi.org/10.1007/978-3-030-45721-1_26

38. Ben-Sasson, E., Bentov, I., Horesh, Y., Riabzev, M.: Scalable zero knowledge with no trusted setup. In: Boldyreva, A., Micciancio, D. (eds.) CRYPTO 2019. LNCS, vol. 11694, pp. 701–732. Springer, Cham (2019). https://doi.org/10.1007/978-3-030-26954-8_23

39. Wahby, R.S., Tzialla, I., Shelat, A., et al.: Doubly-efficient zkSNARKs without trusted setup. In: 2018 IEEE Symposium on Security and Privacy (SP), pp. 926–943. IEEE (2018)

40. Maxwell, G., Poelstra, A., Seurin, Y., et al.: Simple Schnorr multi-signatures with applications to bitcoin. Des. Codes Crypt. **87**(9), 2139–2164 (2019)

41. Ben-Sasson, E., Chiesa, A., Riabzev, M., Spooner, N., Virza, M., Ward, N.P.: Aurora: transparent succinct arguments for R1CS. In: Ishai, Y., Rijmen, V. (eds.) EUROCRYPT 2019. LNCS, vol. 11476, pp. 103–128. Springer, Cham (2019). https://doi.org/10.1007/978-3-030-17653-2_4

42. Chiesa, A., Ojha, D., Spooner, N.: Fractal: post-quantum and transparent recursive proofs from holography. In: Canteaut, A., Ishai, Y. (eds.) EUROCRYPT 2020. LNCS, vol. 12105, pp. 769–793. Springer, Cham (2020). https://doi.org/10.1007/978-3-030-45721-1_27

43. Meiklejohn, S., Pomarole, M., Jordan, G., et al.: A fistful of bitcoins: characterizing payments among men with no names. In: Proceedings of the 2013 Conference on Internet Measurement Conference, pp. 127–140 (2013)

44. Kosba, A., Miller, A., Shi, E., et al.: Hawk: the blockchain model of cryptography and privacy-preserving smart contracts. In: 2016 IEEE Symposium on Security and Privacy (SP), pp. 839–858. IEEE (2016)

45. Maxwell, G.: Confidential transactions (2015). https://people.xiph.org/~greg/confidential_values.txt. Accessed 27 Mar 2019

46. Poelstra, A., Back, A., Friedenbach, M., Maxwell, G., Wuille, P.: Confidential assets. In: Zohar, A., et al. (eds.) FC 2018. LNCS, vol. 10958, pp. 43–63. Springer, Heidelberg (2019). https://doi.org/10.1007/978-3-662-58820-8_4

47. Pedersen, T.P.: Non-interactive and information-theoretic secure verifiable secret sharing. In: Feigenbaum, J. (ed.) CRYPTO 1991. LNCS, vol. 576, pp. 129–140. Springer, Heidelberg (1992). https://doi.org/10.1007/3-540-46766-1_9

48. Ruffing, T., Moreno-Sanchez, P.: ValueShuffle: mixing confidential transactions for comprehensive transaction privacy in bitcoin. In: Brenner, M., et al. (eds.) FC 2017. LNCS, vol. 10323, pp. 133–154. Springer, Cham (2017). https://doi.org/10.1007/978-3-319-70278-0_8

49. Rivest, R.L., Shamir, A., Tauman, Y.: How to leak a secret. In: Boyd, C. (ed.) ASIACRYPT 2001. LNCS, vol. 2248, pp. 552–565. Springer, Heidelberg (2001). https://doi.org/10.1007/3-540-45682-1_32

50. Yu, Z., Au, M.H., Yu, J., Yang, R., Xu, Q., Lau, W.F.: New empirical traceability analysis of CryptoNote-style blockchains. In: Goldberg, I., Moore, T. (eds.) FC 2019. LNCS, vol. 11598, pp. 133–149. Springer, Cham (2019). https://doi.org/10.1007/978-3-030-32101-7_9

51. Noether, S., Mackenzie, A., The Monero Research Lab: Ring confidential transactions. Ledger 1, 1–18 (2016)

52. Kumar, A., Fischer, C., Tople, S., Saxena, P.: A traceability analysis of Monero's blockchain. In: Foley, S.N., Gollmann, D., Snekkenes, E. (eds.) ESORICS 2017. LNCS, vol. 10493, pp. 153–173. Springer, Cham (2017). https://doi.org/10.1007/978-3-319-66399-9_9

53. Ames, S., Hazay, C., Ishai, Y., et al.: Ligero: lightweight sublinear arguments without a trusted setup. In: Proceedings of the 2017 ACM SIGSAC Conference on Computer and Communications Security, pp. 2087–2104 (2017)

54. Feige, U., Lapidot, D., Shamir, A.: Multiple noninteractive zero knowledge proofs under general assumptions. SIAM J. Comput. 29(1), 1–28 (2000)

55. Poelstra, A.: Mimblewimble (2016). http://mimblewimble.cash/20161006-WhitePaperUpdate-e9f45ec.pdf. Accessed 27 Mar 2019

56. Saxena, A., Misra, J., Dhar, A.: Increasing anonymity in bitcoin. In: Böhme, R., Brenner, M., Moore, T., Smith, M. (eds.) FC 2014. LNCS, vol. 8438, pp. 122–139. Springer, Heidelberg (2014). https://doi.org/10.1007/978-3-662-44774-1_9

57. Fuchsbauer, G., Orrù, M., Seurin, Y.: Aggregate cash systems: a cryptographic investigation of mimblewimble. In: Ishai, Y., Rijmen, V. (eds.) EUROCRYPT 2019. LNCS, vol. 11476, pp. 657–689. Springer, Cham (2019). https://doi.org/10.1007/978-3-030-17653-2_22

58. Miers, I., Garman, C., Green, M., Rubin, A.D.: Zerocoin: anonymous distributed e-cash from bitcoin. In: 2013 IEEE Symposium on Security and Privacy, pp. 397–411 (2013)

59. Schnorr, C.P.: Efficient signature generation by smart cards. J. Cryptol. 4(3), 161–174 (1991). https://doi.org/10.1007/BF00196725

60. Ben-Sasson, E., et al.: Zerocash: decentralized anonymous payments from bitcoin. In: 2014 IEEE Symposium on Security and Privacy (SP), pp. 459–474 (2014)

61. Setty, S.: Spartan: efficient and general-purpose zkSNARKs without trusted setup. In: Micciancio, D., Ristenpart, T. (eds.) CRYPTO 2020. LNCS, vol. 12172, pp. 704–737. Springer, Cham (2020). https://doi.org/10.1007/978-3-030-56877-1_25

62. Garman, C., Green, M., Miers, I.: Accountable privacy for decentralized anonymous payments. In: Grossklags, J., Preneel, B. (eds.) FC 2016. LNCS, vol. 9603, pp. 81–98. Springer, Heidelberg (2017). https://doi.org/10.1007/978-3-662-54970-4_5

63. Fauzi, P., Meiklejohn, S., Mercer, R., Orlandi, C.: Quisquis: a new design for anonymous cryptocurrencies. In: Galbraith, S.D., Moriai, S. (eds.) ASIACRYPT 2019. LNCS, vol. 11921, pp. 649–678. Springer, Cham (2019). https://doi.org/10.1007/978-3-030-34578-5_23

64. Bünz, B., Agrawal, S., Zamani, M., Boneh, D.: Zether: towards privacy in a smart contract world. In: Bonneau, J., Heninger, N. (eds.) FC 2020. LNCS, vol. 12059, pp. 423–443. Springer, Cham (2020). https://doi.org/10.1007/978-3-030-51280-4_23

65. Androulaki, E., Camenisch, J., Caro, A.D., Dubovitskaya, M., Elkhiyaoui, K., Tackmann, B.: Privacy-preserving auditable token payments in a permissioned blockchain system. In: Proceedings of the 2nd ACM Conference on Advances in Financial Technologies, AFT 2020, pp. 255–267. Association for Computing Machinery, New York (2020). https://doi.org/10.1145/3419614.3423259

66. Guan, Z., Wan, Z., Yang, Y., Zhou, Y., Huang, B.: Blockmaze: an efficient privacy-preserving account-model blockchain based on zk-SNARKs. IEEE Trans. Dependable Secure Comput. 1 (2020)

67. Shao, W., Jia, C., Xu, Y., Qiu, K., Gao, Y., He, Y.: Attrichain: decentralized traceable anonymous identities in privacy preserving permissioned blockchain. Comput. Secur. **99**, 102069 (2020). http://www.sciencedirect.com/science/article/pii/S0167404820303424

68. Cecchetti, E., Zhang, F., Ji, Y., Kosba, A., Juels, A., Shi, E.: Solidus: confidential distributed ledger transactions via PVORM. In: Proceedings of the 2017 ACM SIGSAC Conference on Computer and Communications Security, CCS 2017, pp. 701–717. Association for Computing Machinery, New York (2017)

69. Wang, X., Ranellucci, S., Katz, J.: Authenticated garbling and efficient maliciously secure two-party computation. In: Proceedings of the 2017 ACM SIGSAC Conference on Computer and Communications Security, pp. 21–37 (2017)

70. Bünz, B., Bootle, J., Boneh, D., et al.: Bulletproofs: short proofs for confidential transactions and more. In: 2018 IEEE Symposium on Security and Privacy (SP), pp. 315–334. IEEE (2018)

71. Bünz, B., Fisch, B., Szepieniec, A.: Transparent SNARKs from DARK compilers. In: Canteaut, A., Ishai, Y. (eds.) EUROCRYPT 2020. LNCS, vol. 12105, pp. 677–706. Springer, Cham (2020). https://doi.org/10.1007/978-3-030-45721-1_24

72. Kilian, J., Petrank, E.: An efficient noninteractive zero-knowledge proof system for NP with general assumptions. J. Cryptol. **11**(1), 1–27 (1998)

73. Boyar, J., Damgard, I., Peralta, R.: Short non-interactive cryptographic proofs. J. Cryptol. **13**(4), 449–472 (2000)

74. Groth, J., Ostrovsky, R., Sahai, A.: Perfect non-interactive zero knowledge for NP. In: Vaudenay, S. (ed.) EUROCRYPT 2006. LNCS, vol. 4004, pp. 339–358. Springer, Heidelberg (2006). https://doi.org/10.1007/11761679_21

75. Gabizon, A., Williamson, Z.J., Ciobotaru, O.: Plonk: permutations over lagrange-bases for oecumenical noninteractive arguments of knowledge. Cryptol. ePrint Arch. (2019)

76. Campanelli, M., Faonio, A., Fiore, D., Querol, A., Rodríguez, H.: Lunar: a toolbox for more efficient universal and updatable zkSNARKs and commit-and-prove extensions. In: Tibouchi, M., Wang, H. (eds.) ASIACRYPT 2021. LNCS, vol. 13092, pp. 3–33. Springer, Cham (2021). https://doi.org/10.1007/978-3-030-92078-4_1

77. Evans, D., Kolesnikov, V., Rosulek, M.: A pragmatic introduction to secure multi-party computation. Found. Trends® Priv. Secur. **2**(2–3), 70–246 (2018)

78. Chase, M., Derler, D., Goldfeder, S., et al.: Post-quantum zero-knowledge and signatures from symmetric-key primitives. In: Proceedings of the 2017 ACM SIGSAC Conference on Computer and Communications Security, pp. 1825–1842 (2017)

79. Katz, J., Kolesnikov, V., Wang, X.: Improved non-interactive zero knowledge with applications to post-quantum signatures. In: Proceedings of the 2018 ACM SIGSAC Conference on Computer and Communications Security, pp. 525–537 (2018)

PCT: A Relay-Based Privacy-Preserving Cross-Chain Transaction Scheme

Da Li[1,2,3], Qinglei Guo[1,2,3], Yansong Wang[4], Shuai Chen[1,2,3], Xiaowen Wu[1,2,3], Lei Wang[4], and Xuan Li[5(✉)]

[1] State Grid Digital Technology Holding Co., Ltd., Beijing 100053, China
[2] State Grid Blockchain Technology (Beijing) Co., Ltd., Beijing 100053, China
[3] Blockchain Technology Laboratory of State Grid Corporation of China, Beijing 100053, China
[4] State Grid Beijing Electric Power Company, Beijing 100031, China
[5] Bubi Technologies Co., Ltd., Beijing 100086, China
leemac1999@163.com

Abstract. Blockchain has been rapidly evolving in recent years and widely used in financial transactions due to its tamper-proof and decentralization features. However, as a relatively independent system, different blockchains have difficulty interoperating with each other, and the issue of "Value Island" becomes more problematic. In addition, the users on the different ledgers are also concerned about the leakage of privacy in the cross-chain process. In this paper, we propose a Privacy-Preserving Cross-Chain Transaction (PCT) scheme combining the relay mechanism with the hash locking mechanism. Meanwhile, the Pedersen commitment is introduced to enable the committers to verify the transaction without acknowledging the amount. We also conduct the range proof based on the Borromean ring signature to ensure that the transaction amount is legitimate. Finally, a lending scheme is designed to solve the problem of insufficient funds in cross-chain transactions. Security analysis and experiments show our scheme achieves privacy-preserving cross-chain transactions with low overhead.

Keywords: Blockchain · Cross-chain · Privacy-preserving · Pedersen commitment · Financial transaction

1 Introduction

As a promising decentralized technology, blockchain technology has been widely used in trustless environments such as the Internet of Things (IoT), the Internet of Vehicles (IoV), energy trading, and medical [1–3]. Driven by the development of Blockchain technology, the distributed cryptocurrency has proliferated and drawn tremendous attention from industries, financial institutions, as well as academia [4]. Blockchain, as a decentralized and trustless ledger with the features of tamper-proof and traceability [5], could avoid the drawbacks brought by traditional centralized trading, such as single point of failure, information opaque, and low operating efficiency [6, 7]. However, there are

Y. Sun et al. (Eds.): CBCC 2022, CCIS 1736, pp. 83–99, 2022.
https://doi.org/10.1007/978-981-19-8877-6_6

lots of heterogeneous blockchains equipped with different access strategies, consensus mechanisms, and block structures co-existing, making it hard to communicate or trade between various blockchains [8]. "Value Island" is gradually forming, limiting the synergistic effect between industries that could have been brought by the development of blockchain to a great extent [9].

In order to improve the interoperation of distributed ledger, the research on Cross-Chain Technology (CCT) has been a key direction in the field of blockchain. Interledger [10] is a representative of a cross-chain protocol using the notary scheme. Interledger uses connectors to transfer transactions across systems, and the assets will be locked by all systems in the transmission line. Pegged sidechains [11] were firstly proposed based on "two-way peg" and aimed to realize the transfer of different blockchain assets without affecting the main chain. Poon et al. designed Plasma [12] based on the sidechain, while other cross-chain projects Cosmos [13], polkadot [14], and BTC-Relay [15] all reflect the idea of relay [16]. Hash locking first appeared in Bitcoin Lightning network [17], which conducts the zero-confirmation transactions using the hashed time-locked smart contract. These schemes realize the cross-chain transfer of assets and information to a certain degree. However, they do not consider the protection of sensitive information in the process of cross-chain transactions.

There are also several distributed privacy-preserving technologies such as Zerocoin [18], Coinjoin [19], and zkLedger [20] that designed to conduct the privacy-preserving transactions in blockchain. However, most of the above only target one decentralized ledger. Due to a lack of uniform standards, these methods cannot be applied to the cross-chain protocol. Raze network [21] protects the users' privacy in the cross-chain transaction with Raze bridge, but the adversaries still can acquire the details of transactions by eavesdropping on the information from the bridge. Deshpande et al. [22] explore the different notions of privacy in anonymity, confidentiality, and indistinguishability of the cross-chain process, but the scheme only works for atomic swaps between two parties. How to break "Value Island" and realize the privacy-preserving cross-chain transaction between multi-parties is one of the most significant directions in the blockchain.

Under the circumstances, we design a Privacy-Preserving Cross-Chain Transaction (PCT) scheme. Our contributions are as follows:

1. We propose a relay-based cross-chain transaction scheme among multi-parties combining with Pedersen commitment, the legal verification of the transactions could be performed without leaking any trading details.
2. The core idea of hash locking is introduced to help ensure the fairness of the transaction. Additionally, we develop the Borromean ring signature to perform the range proof of hidden amount.
3. A supplementary lending scheme is also designed to face the situation of users' lack of assets in the process of cross-chain transactions.

2 Preliminaries

2.1 Cross-Chain Technology

Cross-Chain Technology (CCT) realizes information exchange and assets transfer from one ledger to another, improving the scalability and the interoperability of blockchain. CCT aims to realize 1) Atomic transfer of assets between different blockchains. 2) Locking and unlocking of assets on one ledger 3) Verification of transaction status on other ledgers. The changes between the two ledgers need to be consistent under the premise of conservation of value. From a technical perspective, there are four primary categories of strategies for CCT: notary schemes, sidechains/relays, hash locking, and distributed privacy key control.

- Notary schemes assume that the notary is a trusted group, like the intermediary in the real world, that can listen for and respond to transaction requests or events actively or passively. The security depends primarily on the notary.
- Sidechains/relays perform the collection, verification, and forwarding of messages through the execution of smart contracts, which can be viewed as the extension of the main chain. Relay technology is the most mature and widely used CCT, whose core idea is to construct a third public chain between different blockchains.
- Hash locking realizes the cross-chain communication and transaction through executing the specific smart contracts. There are two well-designed contracts: Revocable Sequence Maturity Contract (RSMC) and Hashed Timelock Contract (HTLC). The former requires the parties to sign for the trading, while the latter guarantees the atomicity of transactions.
- Distributed private key control introduces the multi-party computation and threshold key to the cross-chain process. Ownership and access to digital assets are separated by distributed controlling the private key.

2.2 Pedersen Commitment

Pedersen commitment [23] has two properties, hiding and blinding, respectively. Hiding means that the generated commitment will not leak any information of original value. Blinding refers to the commitment and the original value is a one-to-one correspondence, the user who generated the commitment cannot change the value when opening the commitment. The construction of Pedersen commitment based on the Elliptic Curve is as follows:

- Initialization: Determine the elliptic curve and select the two base points G and H of the order of the large prime p on the elliptic curve as common parameters. During the process, the selection of H needs to be well-designed under the premise of not leaking any secrets, which prevents the malicious nodes from stealing more revenue [24].

– Generate the commitment: The commitment party selects a blinding factor r randomly, and computes the corresponding commitment cm of the original message v, then the result will be sent to the receiver:

$$cm(v, r) = v \cdot G + r \cdot H \tag{1}$$

– Open the commitment: The receiver uses the original value v and the blinding factor r provided by the commitment party to perform the commitment generation process again. If the result is equal to cm, then the commitment can be considered legal.

Pedersen commitment has the property of additive homomorphism. If $cm_1 = cm(v_1, r_1) = v_1 \cdot G + r_1 \cdot H, cm_2 = cm(v_2, r_2) = v_2 \cdot G + r_2 \cdot H$ then:

$$\begin{aligned} cm_1 + cm_2 &= (v_1 \cdot G + r_1 \cdot H) + (v_2 \cdot G + r_2 \cdot H) \\ &= (v_1 + v_2) \cdot G + (r_1 + r_2) \cdot H \\ &= cm(v_1 + v_2, r_1 + r_2) \end{aligned} \tag{2}$$

2.3 Ring Signature

Ring signature [25] is a signing algorithm that could hide the signer in a group, which is widely used in environments that require authentication and anonymity [26]. In a general way, the public keys of other members in the group are used repeatedly to generate a ring, and the private key of the signer is used in the final closed-loop step, so as to achieve the indistinguishability of the signer.

Borromean ring signature [27], constructed by Schnorr authentication [28], AOS ring signature [29], and hash function, is a multi-rings signature technology which is spatially optimized compared to a single ring signature.

3 System Architecture and Models

We introduce the relay mechanism to realize value transferring cross chains and propose a privacy-preserving supported cross-chain transaction scheme based on the Pedersen commitment. During the whole phase of the transaction, none of the nodes can acquire the specific amount of the transaction except the participants, which can protect the privacy of the participants to the utmost extent. The committer nodes in the blockchain networks verify the legality of the transaction by calculating the Pedersen commitment.

In this section, we will present our system architecture and the transaction models deployed on the blockchain. The architecture of our scheme is shown in Fig. 1.

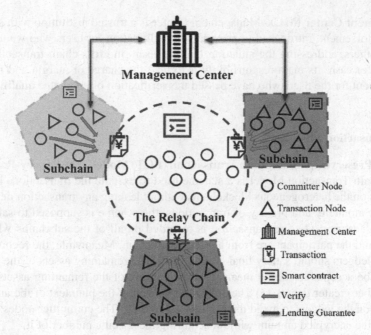

Fig. 1. Architecture of PCT

3.1 System Roles

In our system, **relay chain** is utilized to take the record of cross-chain transactions and all the other ledgers are called **subchains.** Nodes in the blockchain network can generally be classified into two types, committer nodes, and transaction nodes. A node can act as both a committer node and a transaction node at the same time.

Transaction Nodes. The transaction nodes consist of the initiator and the participant. The initiator is the payer of the transaction. There is only one initiator in a transaction. However, there may exist multiple participants in a transaction. The initiator is responsible for initiating a transaction and generating the transaction record. After receiving the record, the participants in the transaction verify the amount of it and sign with their private keys to show their approval.

Committer Nodes. The committer nodes are in charge of maintaining the ledger on the blockchain. After transaction legality verification and remaining assets range proof, the transaction record will be committed by the committer nodes and recorded on the ledgers. To realize the privacy-preserving transaction process, the amount of the transaction is never revealed to the committer nodes. In our system, committer nodes on the relay chain (CNr) and on the subchains (CNs-A refers to committer nodes on subchain A) have different access control rights. The records on the ledger of the relay chain are available to the committers on the subchains (CNs). On the contrary, the records on the subchains are only revealed to the committers on the relay chain (CNr) and the subchains (CNs) where the records are stored.

Management Center (MC). Management Center is a trusted institution with a certain credit endorsement, introduced to provide the qualification for users who want to lend cash to others, addressing the situation that the users in cross-chain transactions are strapped for cash. Its main responsibility is to take the charge of margin and make an endorsement for the users who have passed the verification of guarantee qualification.

3.2 Transaction Models

Privacy-Preserving Cross-Chain Transaction (PCT) Model. The Privacy-Preserving Cross-Chain Transaction Model is a scheme used to execute the transactions between the nodes on the heterogeneous blockchains without leaking any transaction details. To guarantee atomicity and privacy of transactions, the scheme is supposed to satisfy the following features: (1) The transaction is recorded on all of the subchains where the initiator and the participant are from and the relay chain. Meanwhile, the record on the different ledgers should satisfy final certainty. (2) The remaining assets of the initiator ought to be acceptable, which means that the amount of the remaining assets should be a number greater than 0. (3) The ciphertext instead of the plaintext of the amount is recorded on the ledgers to avoid the privacy leakage. (4) The committer nodes are able to verify the encrypted amount without acquiring the specific number of it.

In our scheme, the Pedersen commitment is used to encrypt transaction amount to hide it from committer nodes. Furthermore, for the purpose of anonymity, irrelevant nodes can be involved in the transaction, whose amount will be set as 0. The relay mechanism is introduced to allow value to cross the barriers between chains, so that the value originally stored on a specific chain is converted to the value on another chain, thereby realizing the circulation of value.

Lending Transaction Model. The lending transaction model is designed to eliminate the probability that the initiator has difficulties in the turnover of capital to a certain degree. When meeting the problem of financing, the initiator can borrow money from the guaranteed user who gains the qualification to lend money from the Management Center (MC). And the money borrowed from the guaranteed user can be transferred between chains as prior.

4 Privacy-Preserving Cross-Chain Transaction Scheme (PCT)

4.1 Cross-Chain Transaction

Our scheme can realize the multi-parties cross-chain transaction. Assume that the subchain where the initiator P_a is located is subchain A and the subchains set in which the other participants $\mathbb{P}_b = \{P_{b1}, P_{b2}, \cdots, P_{bk}\}$ are located is $\mathbb{B}$. The thorough process of PCT consists of four parts: the **Nodes Initialization**, the **Transaction Negotiation**, the **Range Proof**, and the **Transaction Process**.

Nodes Initialization. Once a new node applies to join the blockchain network, the system will execute the assets authentication by verifying the assets v_0 that the user claims. After passing the access mechanism of the blockchain, the node is about to join in. Following the assets authentication, the system will generate a blinding factor (randomness) r_0 for the node. Then the Pedersen commitment of v_0 is automatically calculated by the smart contract and recorded as the first transaction of the user. The Pedersen commitment of v_0 can be calculated utilizing the public parameters G, H as follows:

$$cm_0 = v_0 G + r_0 H \tag{3}$$

After the above steps, the node successfully joins the blockchain network.

Transaction Negotiation. Due to the heterogeneity of various blockchains, there exist dramatic differences in the data structure and the exchange rate between the currency on different blockchain systems. On the stage of transaction negotiation, our system completes the currency value exchange according to the exchange rate between different subchains and generates transaction records that will be written on the ledgers later.

(1) The transaction initiator P_a on the subchain A calculates the encrypted amount V_A in $V_A = v_A G$ and broadcasts the request R_A attached with V_A to all the nodes in the system. He then generates the blinding factor r_A for himself and r_x for each participant P_{bx} of the transaction, making sure that $r_A + \sum r_x = 0$. The format of R_A is as follows:

$$R_A = <Users, V_A, TS, C_r = \{E_{pk_{b1}}(r_1), \cdots , E_{pk_{bk}}(r_k)\}, Sign_{sk_a}(User_a)>$$

where $Users$ is the set of transaction participants, TS is the timestamp of the transaction, C_r denotes the blinding factors encrypted by the public keys of the transaction participants $\mathbb{P}_b$, $Sign_{sk_a}(User_a)$ is the digital signature of P_a's identification signed by the private key of P_a. And only the public key of P_a can decrypt the signature.

(2) After collecting the request R_A, the transaction participant $P_{bx}(x \in [1, k])$ in $\mathbb{P}_b$ obtains the blinding factor r_x by decrypting $E_{pk_{bx}}(r_x)$ with his own private key. Then he broadcasts the confirming message C_{Bx} to respond to the request. The message includes the signature of R_A and the encrypted amount $V_{Bx} = v_{Bx} G$ that P_{bx} desires to get from P_a in the currency on the subchain B_x. C_{Bx} is generated as follows:

$$C_{Bx} = <User_{bx}, R_A, V_{Bx}, TS, Sign_{bx}(R_A||User_{bx})>$$

where $User_{bx}$ stands for the identification of the transaction participant P_{bx}, R_A is the transaction request from P_a, TS is the timestamp of the transaction and $Sign_{bx}(R_A||User_{bx})$ denotes the signature of the message which is the concatenation of R_A and $User_{bx}$.

(3) Once CNr collect both the request and the confirming message, the smart contract deployed on the relay chain will be triggered to complete the value transfer according to the exchange rate between the subchain A and the subchain $Bx \in \mathbb{B}$. And the smart contract automatically verifies whether the equation

$x_{A \to Bx} V_A = x_{A \to Bx} v_A G = -v_{Bx} G = V_{Bx}$ is true, where $x_{A \to Bx}$ represents the exchange rate between the currency. If the equality is established, the transaction participants reach a consensus on the amount of the transaction and the nodes on the relay chain will send $\mathbb{V}_B = \{V_{B1}, \cdots V_{Bk}\}$ to P_a.

(4) The transaction initiator P_a calculate the Pedersen commitments of v_A and $\mathbb{V}_B$ after obtaining $x_{A \to Bx}^{-1} V_{Bx}(x \in [1, k])$, where $x_{A \to Bx}^{-1} \cdot x_{A \to Bx} = 1$:

$$cm_A = V_A + r_A H = v_A G + rH \tag{4}$$

$$cm_{Bx} = -x_{A \to Bx}^{-1} V_{Bx} + r_x H = -v_A G + r_x H, x \in [1, k] \tag{5}$$

Finally, the transaction record Tx is generated:

$$Tx = <ID, Users, Cmts, TS, Sign_{sk_a}(ID)>$$

where ID denotes the uniquely identifies, $Users$ is the set of transaction participants, $Cmts$ denotes the set of Pedersen commitments, TS is the timestamp of the transaction, the $Sign_{sk_a}(ID)$ is the digital signature of ID signed by the private key of P_a.

Range Proof. IN this paper, the verification processes during the transaction are based on the additively homomorphism of the Pedersen commitments. And all addition operations are modulo-N based on groups of integers of order N, which brings the problem that the amount of transaction may overflow. Consequently, the malicious nodes can illegitimately create a numerous amount of assets by exploiting the vulnerability that adding a larger number is equivalent to subtracting a small one. However, illegal transactions can hardly be detected. Therefore, it is a big deal to make sure that the committed values are within an acceptable range.

In our scheme, the range proof based on the Borromean ring signature is introduced to guarantee the legality of the Pedersen commitment. The whole process consists of two phases, the generating phase and the verifying phase.

Generation Phase. Note that if v is the value to be committed, r is the selected blinding factor, and $cm = vG + rH$ denotes the Pedersen commitment of v, the process of the generating phase is as follows:

(1) Calculate the Pedersen commitment of v:

$$cm = vG + rH \tag{6}$$

(2) Represent v in binary form. And each bit has two possible values, "0" and "1". Therefore, to construct the Borromean ring signature for v, we take the conjunction of $n = 32$ rings, and each ring has $m = 2$ signature members. Each member has his corresponding public key $Pk_{i,j}$ where $i \in [1, 32], j \in \{0, 1\}[1, 32], j \in \{0, 1\}$, but only one member has the real private key $r_{i,j}$. Note that $r_{i,j}$ meets $\sum_{i=1}^{n} r_{i,j} = r$.

(3) Calculate the hash value of v:

$$M = H(v) \tag{7}$$

where $H(\cdot)$ denotes the one-way hash function.

(4) According to the representation of v in binary form, determine a set of unknown but fixed $\{j_i^*\}_0^{n-1}$, where j_i^* is the value of v's i th bit.

(5) For each $0 \le i \le n - 1$:

1) Choose a scalar k_i uniformly at random.
2) Set $e_{i,j_i^*+1} = H(M\,||k_iG||i||j_i^*)$
3) If $j_i^* = 1$, choose $s_{i,0}$ at random and compute:

$$e_{i,0} = H(M\,||s_{i,0}G - e_{i,0}Pk_{i,0}||i||0) \tag{8}$$

(6) Compute $e_0 = H(s_{0,1}G - e_{0,1}Pk_{0,1}||\ldots||s_{n-1,1}G - e_{n-1,1}Pk_{n-1,1})$. The calculation of e_0 includes the values of signatures $\{s_{i,0}\}_{i=0}^{n-1}$.

(7) For $0 \le i \le n - 1$, compute $s_{i,j_i^*} = k_i + r_i e_{i,j_i^*}$.

(8) The signature of v is $\delta = \{e_0, s_{i,j} : 0 \le i \le n - 1, 0 \le j \le m - 1\}$

(9) To prove the committed value is in a legal range, one can send both the Pedersen commitment and the signature of v to others.

Verification Phase. Since verification does not depend on which specific keys are known, the range of v can be verified without revealing the specific value of v. The verifiers can verify whether the commitment is in a legal range with the following steps:

(1) Validate whether Eq. (9) is established:

$$cm = \sum_{i=0}^{n-1} cm_i \tag{9}$$

where $cm_i = v_iG + r_iH$ denotes the Pedersen Commitment of each bit of v.

(2) Validate whether Eq. (10) is established:

$$e_0' = H(R_{0,m_0}||\ldots||R_{n,m_0}) = e_0 \tag{10}$$

where $R_{i,j+1} = s_{i,j}G + e_{i,j}P_{i,j}$ and $e_{i,j} = H(M\,||R_{i,j+1}||i||j + 1)$.

(3) It means that the committed value is in a legal range, if Eq. (9) and Eq. (10) are true at the same time

On account for the one-to-one correspondence between the committed values and the blinding factors, only the right value can conduct the Borromean ring signature. Thanks to the properties of the ring signature, the verifiers can validate the value without acquiring the exact number of the value. There exists little probability for the malicious nodes to conduct the blinding factor for the value which is smaller than 0 and whose signature is the same as the signature conducted by the real one. In this way, we finish the range proof of the hidden amount.

Transaction Process. During the transaction process, to prevent double-spending, the hash lock and the time lock are introduced to our scheme. As shown in Fig. 2, the transaction process consists of 8 steps.

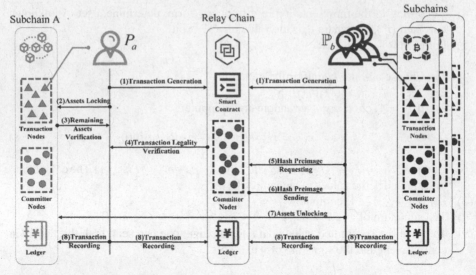

Fig. 2. The transaction process of cross-chain transaction

(1) Transaction Generation: Generate the transaction record Tx following the steps in **Transaction Negotiation.**

(2) Assets Locking: After receiving the transaction record in the prior step, the smart contract deployed on the relay chain generates a hash preimage set S. Each $s_i \in S$ denotes the hash preimage of a part of the assets which is corresponding to a transaction participant. Meanwhile, the time lock is set. The assets are locked on the subchain A unless the correct preimage is provided in a limited time T. And it will be returned to P_a, if it is not unlocked in T.

(3) Remaining Assets Verification: After locking the assets of P_a, CNs-A make the range proof of the remaining assets of P_a. The detail of range proof is provided in **Range Proof.**

(4) Transaction Legality Verification: The CNr verify the legality of the transaction Tx by computing $\sum cm$, where $cm \in Cmts$. Given that $\sum r = 0$, then if $\sum cm = 0$, we can infer that $\sum v = 0$ according to the $\sum cm = \sum v \cdot G + \sum r \cdot H$. So the committer nodes only need to consider whether $\sum cm = 0$ as a measure of whether the transaction is legal. Once the verification passes, CNr write the ID of the transaction on the relay chain. Note that the record does not mean that the transaction has been completed.

(5) Hash Preimage Requesting: When the CNS-$\mathbb{B}$ listen that the related transaction has been recorded on the relay chain, they verify the legality of transaction. The transaction participants in $\mathbb{P}_b$ then request the hash preimage $s_i \in S$ from the relay chain to unlock the part of P_a's assets on the subchain A he deserved.

(6) Hash Preimage Sending: After receiving all the requests from P_{bx}, the corresponding hash preimage are sent to P_{bx} by the relay chain.

(7) Assets Unlocking: Each participant in $\mathbb{P}_b$ utilizes the hash preimage $s_i \in S$ obtained from the prior step to unlock the assets he deserved in the transaction.

(8) Transaction Recording: The committers of the subchains verify the commitments and record the transaction *Tx* on their ledger. Finally, the CNr mark the transaction *Tx* as *Done*. A cross-chain transaction is completed.

For the purpose of ensuring the atomicity of the transaction, the record *Tx* will be marked as *Failed* in the following situations:

a. The range proof of the remaining assets in step (3) failed.
b. The sum of the Pedersen commitments is not 0 in step (4).
c. The assets are not unlocked within the limited time.
d. The transaction record *Tx* is not recorded on the any ledgers of the subchains.

4.2 Lending Transaction

During cross-chain transactions, there exists an open question that the payer may have difficulties in lacking enough assets to finish the transaction. To deal with the problem of turnover of capital, the lending business is indispensable. A privacy-preserving lending transaction based on the Pedersen commitment is proposed in our scheme, as shown in Fig. 3. We introduce the Management Center (MC), which takes charge of providing qualifications to the nodes called guarantee providers. After paying the margin, the guarantee providers can provide loan service to the node which is lack of assets.

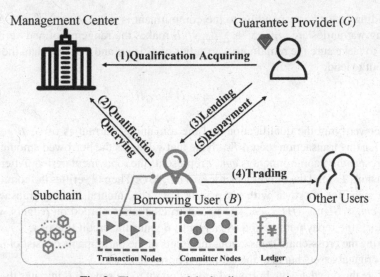

Fig. 3. The process of the lending transaction

When transaction participants meet the cash-flow problem, the process of the lending transaction is as follows:

(1) The guarantee provider G transfers the margin v, also the amount of guarantee he apply for, to the MC. And the lending guarantee record Tx_v is generated:

$$Tx_v = <ID, Users_v, Cmts_v, TS, Sign_{skG}(ID, cm_v)>$$

where ID is the lending transaction identification, $Users_v$ is the set of participants $\{G, MC\}$, $Cmts_v$ denotes the set of commitments $\{cm(-v, -r_v), cm(v, r_v)\}$.

After being recorded on the ledger by the committers, the guarantee transaction will be sent to MC. Then MC signs the record with its private key, and G gets the qualification to lend money. Meanwhile, the record Tx_v is collected in secured transaction collection (STC) in MC and the query indices are available to all the nodes.

(2) The user B who borrows money verifies the qualification of G:

1) Query the transaction record which is provided by G in STC.
2) Make sure that G is able to provide capital. Assume that the sum of the number of lending transactions provided by G is m. B gathers the commitments in Tx_v and executes the calculation:

$$cm_G = cm_v + \sum_{i=1}^{m} cm_i \tag{11}$$

The blinding factor corresponding to the commitment is $r_G = r_v + \sum_{i=1}^{m} r_i$. And the remaining warranties are $v_G = v + \sum_{i=1}^{m} v_i$. B makes the range proof and verifies the Eq. (12) to make sure the remaining warranties of G is v_G and is larger than the money he is about to lend.

$$cm_G = v_G G + r_G H \tag{12}$$

(3) After verifying the qualification and the remaining warranties of G, B generates the lending transaction record Tx_s. Note that s denotes the borrowed amount whose corresponding commitment is cm_s, t represents the repayment period. After that, B transmits Tx_s and the blinding factor r_s of cm_s to G. Then G verifies the commitment and signs for approval with his private key. The integral lending transaction $< ID, cm_s, t, Sign_{skG}(ID, t, cm_s) >$ is constructed and recorded on ledgers, where t denotes the repayment period. As a result, B gains the credit line of s.
(4) During the cross-chain transaction, the assets of the participants consist of not only his original assets but also the capital he borrowed.
(5) Before the due date, the borrowed money ought to be repaid. B initiates the repayment transaction and add the signature attached with the repaid tag RI to the lending transaction Tx_s:$Sign_{skB}(ID, RI)$.Then G updates his warranties.

5 Security Analysis

5.1 Anonymity

We ensure the anonymity of the transaction by introducing the irrelevant participants to hide the transaction parties in a group. They don't need to take the risk of asset theft cause the amount that they made for the commitment is 0. From the perspective of the initiator, he can make the transactions more covert at the little cost of generating some additional blinding factors. Because other committer nodes cannot distinguish the spender, the receiver or the irrelevant participant of the transaction through the commitment, PCT can protect the users' privacy effectively.

5.2 Confidentiality

WE adopt Elliptic-Curve-based Pedersen commitment to guarantee the confidentiality of transaction amount. Transaction participants do not record the payment details on the ledger. Instead, they only need to publish the commitment. We can reduce the security of Pedersen commitment to the hardness of elliptic curve discrete logarithm problem (ECDLP) and elliptic curve decisional Diffie–Hellman problem (ECDDHP). Attackers cannot infer the specific amount under the premise that they only know G, H and cm. Additionally, the committer nodes also have no idea about the original value as they do not need to open the commitment but only verify if $\sum cm = 0$ utilizing the additive homomorphism nature of Pedersen commitment [20].

5.3 Reliability

WE use the Borromean ring signature to improve the reliability of PCT on the basis of Confidentiality. We map the acceptable range of assets to a signers' group, and the verifiers could only verify that the signer (the specific value) is in the group (valid range) but they cannot distinguish the signer according to the nature of ring signature. The supplementary range proof can avoid malicious nodes creating illegal assets, so as to ensure the security of the transaction.

6 Experiments

WE now present the empirical results for the privacy-preserving cross-chain transaction scheme. In Sect. 6.1, we demonstrate the time cost and the storage cost of the range proof based on the Borromean ring signature. In Sect. 6.2, we investigate the performance of the Pedersen commitment generation and verification during the transaction process. Our experimental environment includes a Windows11 operating system running on an AMD Ryzen 6 3600 processor at 3200 MHz with 16 GB of memory.

Table 1. Time cost of the range proof

Phase		Executed time
Generation phase	Commitment generating	139.13 ms
	Key generating	163.14 ms
	Signature generating	257.23 ms
Verification phase	Commitment verifying	5.00 ms
	Signature verifying	344.31 ms

6.1 The Performance of Commitment Range Proof

IN our scheme, the range proof mainly consists of the signature generation phase and the signature verification phase. We evaluate the time cost and the storage cost of the two phases respectively. We execute each phase 20 times and obtain its average time to analyze the performance. The results of this execution are shown in Table 1.

As shown in Table 1, the time cost of the generation phase is the sum of the time cost of the commitment generating, the key generating, and signing, that is $139.13 + 163.14 + 257.23 = 559.50$ ms. As for the verification phase, the time cost is $344.31 + 5.00 = 349.31$ ms. For the whole process, the generation phase is only executed by the initiator and the verification phase is executed by the committers.

Table 2. Storage cost of the range proof

Item	Count	Storage cost
Private key	32	2 KB
Public key	64	4 KB
Pedersen commitment	33	4.125 KB

We also analyze the storage cost of the range proof. As shown in Table 2, it respectively takes 2 KB, 4 KB, and 4.125 KB space to store the private keys, the public keys, and the commitments of the amount. Considering the necessity of the range proof, the time cost and the storage cost are acceptable.

6.2 The Performance of Transaction Generation and Verification

TO evaluate the performance of the time cost of the transaction generation and verification, we simulate the situation with different numbers of transaction nodes to investigate how the time cost varies with the increasement of the nodes amount. We perform the experiments with the node numbers of 2, 5, 10, 15, 20, 25, 30, 35, 40, 45, 50 respectively. The results are shown in Fig. 4 and Fig. 5.

As shown in Fig. 3, the time cost of transaction generation basically increases linearly with the number of nodes. The greater the number of nodes participating in the

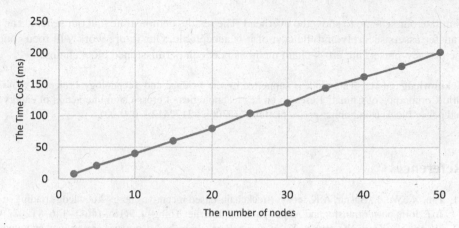

Fig. 4. The variation of the transaction generation time cost with different node numbers

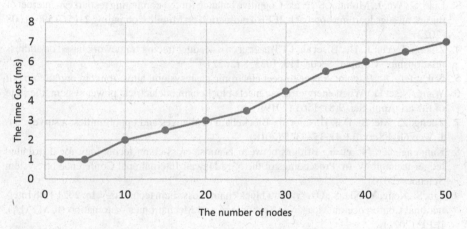

Fig. 5. The variation of the transaction verification time cost with different node numbers

transaction, the greater the time cost. Compared to the time cost of generation, the time cost of verification is much smaller. Overall, the time cost of the transaction is acceptable since the transaction generation is only executed by the initiator and the transaction verifications are executed by multiple committers in the network.

7 Conclusion

In this paper, we propose a privacy-preserving cross-chain transaction (PCT) scheme based on the relay mechanism. Aiming at the problem of privacy protection, we introduce the Pedersen commitment to hide the specific amount of the transaction. Meanwhile, the range proof based on the Borromean ring signature is combined in our scheme to avoid the creation of illegal assets. We also provide a lending transaction scheme to solve the problem in the turnover of capital. Finally, we analyze the security of our scheme and simulate our scheme to show the overhead. The results demonstrate that our scheme can transfer assets securely and the cost of it is acceptable. Our future work will focus on the privacy-preserving cross-chain methods between permissioned blockchains.

Acknowledgements. This work is supported by the Science and Technology Project of State Grid Corporation of China: "Research on key technologies of cross-chain interaction of energy and power blockchain public service platform" (5700-202172412A-0–0-00).

References

1. Lin, X., Wu, J., Bashir, A.K., et al.: Blockchain-based incentive energy-knowledge trading in IoT: Joint power transfer and AI design. IEEE Internet Things J. **9**(16), 14685–14698 (2022)
2. Wang, N., Yang, W., Wang, X., et al.: A blockchain based privacy-preserving federated learning scheme for Internet of vehicles. Digital Commun. Netw. (2022)
3. Liao, S., Wu, J., Mumtaz, S., et al.: Cognitive balance for fog computing resource in internet of things: an edge learning approach. IEEE Transaction on Mobile Computing **21**(5), 1596–1608 (2022)
4. Zhang, Z., Yin, J., Hu, B., et al.: CLTracer: a cross-ledger tracing framework based on address relationships. Comput. Secur. **113**, 102558 (2022)
5. Nakamoto, S.: Bitcoin: A peer-to-peer electronic cash system. https://bitcoin.org/bitcoin.pdf
6. Wang, N., et al.: When energy trading meets blockchain in electrical power system: the state of the art. Appl. Sci. **9**(8), 1561 (2019)
7. Zheng, Z., Xie, S., Dai, H.N., et al.: Blockchain challenges and opportunities: a survey. Int. J. Web Grid Serv. **14**(4), 352–375 (2018)
8. Kannengießer, N., et al.: Bridges between islands: cross-chain technology for distributed ledger technology. In: Proceedings of the 53rd Hawaii International Conference on System Sciences (2020)
9. Lin, S., Kong, Y., Nie, S.: Overview of block chain cross chain technology. In: 2021 13th International Conference on Measuring Technology and Mechatronics Automation (ICMTMA). IEEE (2021)
10. Hope-Bailie, A., Thomas, S.: Interledger: creating a standard for payments. In: Proceedings of the 25th International Conference Companion on World Wide Web (2016)
11. Back, A., Corallo, M., Dashjr, L., et al.: Enabling blockchain innovations with pegged sidechains. **72**, 201—224 (2014) http://www.opensciencereview.com/papers/123/enablingblockchain-innovations-with-pegged-sidechains
12. Poon, J., Buterin, V.: Plasma: scalable autonomous smart contracts. White Pap. 1–47 (2017)
13. Kwon, J., Buchman, E.: A network of distributed ledgers. Cosmos, dated, 1–41, (2018)
14. Wood, G.: Polkadot: vision for a heterogeneous multi-chain framework. White Pap. **21** (2016)
15. ConsenSys. BTC Relay's documentation. http://btc-relay.readthedocs.io/en/latest/
16. Dilley, J., Poelstra, A., Wilkins, J., et al.: Strong federations: an interoperable blockchain solution to centralized third-party risks. arXiv:1612.05491 (2016)
17. Poon, J., Dryja, T.: The bitcoin lightning network: scalable off-chain instant payments (2016)
18. Miers, I., Garman, C., Green, M., et al.: Zerocoin: anonymous distributed E-Cash from bitcoin. In: 2013 IEEE Symposium on Security and Privacy (SP). IEEE (2013)
19. Maxwell, G.: CoinJoin: bitcoin privacy for the real world.post on bitcoin forum (2013)
20. Narula, N., Vasquez, W., Virza, M.: zkledger: privacy-preserving auditing for distributed ledgers. In: 15th {USENIX} Symposium on Networked Systems Design and Implementation ({NSDI} 18), 65–80 (2018). Author, F.: Article title. Journal **2**(5), 99–110 (2016)

21. Network, R.: Trustless Privacy on Polkadot. https://www.raze.network
22. Deshpande, A., Maurice, H.: Privacy-preserving cross-chain atomic swaps. In: International Conference on Financial Cryptography and Data Security. Springer, Cham (2020)
23. Pedersen, T.P.: Non-interactive and information theoretic secure verifiable secret sharing. In: Proceedings of the 11th Annual International Cryptology Conference (1992), CRYPTO 1991, pp. 129–140 (1992)
24. Gibson, A.: An investigation into confidential transactions, vol. 93 (2016). https://github.com/AdamISZ/ConfidentialTransactionsDoc/blob/master/essayonCT.pdf.
25. Rivest, R.L., Shamir, A., Tauman, Y.: How to leak a secret. In: International conference on the theory and application of cryptology and information security, pp. 552–565. Springer, Berlin, Heidelberg (2001)
26. Yang, W., Wang, N., Guan, Z., et al.: IEEE Wireless Communications (2022)
27. Maxwell, G., Poelstra, A.: Borromean ring signatures (2015). Accessed 8 June 2019
28. Schnorr, C.P.: Efficient identification and signatures for smart cards. In: Conference on the Theory and Application of Cryptology, pp. 239–252. Springer, New York (1989)
29. Abe, M., Ohkubo, M., Suzuki, K.: 1-out-of-n signatures from a variety of keys. In: International Conference on the Theory and Application of Cryptology and Information Security, pp. 415–432. Springer, Berlin, (2002)

An Illegal Data Supervision Scheme for the Consortium Blockchain

Xiqin Wang[1], Kun Zhang[2], Yong Ding[1], Fang Yuan[3], Hai Liang[1(✉)], and Changsong Yang[1]

[1] Guilin University of Electronic Technology, Guilin 541004, China
lianghai@guet.edu.cn
[2] State Information Center, Beijing 100000, China
[3] Communications Bureau of the Ministry of Foreign Affairs, Beijing 100000, China

Abstract. With the rapid development of blockchain, many enterprise-level applications have used consortium blockchain to ensure the system's immutability and decentralization. However, due to the immutability of blockchain, the cost of removing illegal data on the blockchain is relatively high. Although the permission blockchain has restricted users' actions, there will still be illegal data on the chain, which brings great regulatory difficulties to the government. Therefore, how to efficiently supervise the blockchain has become an important issue. In this article, in order to supervise illegal data with different impacts, we propose a hierarchical blocking scheme for illegal data in consortium blockchain. First, for illegal data with little impact, we use regular expressions on the application side to prevent users from accessing illegal data. Second, the smart contract can be used by supervisors to mark illegal data with greater impact. The experimental results show the effectiveness and practicability of our scheme.

Keywords: Consortium blockchain · Illegal data · Supervision · Regular expressions · Smart contract · Access control

1 Introduction

Nakamoto [15] proposed the concept of blockchain and created the Bitcoin social network in 2009. He developed the first block, and the blockchain began to appear in front of the world. Peer-to-peer and distributed timestamp servers enable blockchain databases to be managed autonomously [4]. The characteristics of decentralization, anonymity, autonomy, openness, and traceability of the blockchain make it possible to integrate with many applications. In particular, the decentralized characteristics of the blockchain enable it to establish a peer-to-peer trustworthy value transfer with strange nodes without relying on third-party. The various characteristics of the blockchain can reduce transaction costs and improve interaction efficiency. Therefore, the blockchain has a very broad application prospect [25]. Many fields such as finance, energy, and medical care can be combined with blockchain for applications. Combining blockchain for application innovation has become the current development trend [16].

Y. Sun et al. (Eds.): CBCC 2022, CCIS 1736, pp. 100–115, 2022.
https://doi.org/10.1007/978-981-19-8877-6_7

As an emerging internet technology, blockchain has been applied in various fields and developed into a new model under the modern sharing economy. Unlike the traditional transaction model, transactions on the blockchain can be carried out without a third party. Some criminals have taken advantage of the opportunities of this era and use blockchain as a tool for crimes in various fields to do things that violate the law [20]. However, a large amount of data on the blockchain may face the problem of difficult data management and the proliferation of illegal data [24]. The immutability of the blockchain makes the supervision of blockchain data a difficult problem. It will cause extremely serious consequences if all kinds of illegal data that are expressly prohibited by laws and regulations are allowed to spread on the blockchain [5]. Therefore, to avoid this kind of thing, the author needs to consider how to supervise the data on the blockchain [2].

The consortium blockchain is a specific blockchain that allows authorized nodes to maintain a distributed sharing database. The consortium blockchain has good application cases in the fields of finance, law, medical care, and energy [12]. For the information prohibited by laws and administrative regulations, the consortium blockchain should have the immediate and emergency response capabilities of publishing, recording, storing, and disseminating [8]. Therefore, for the data existing on the consortium blockchain, the author should consider dealing with illegal data so that the user cannot access them. Although the supervision of consortium blockchain has achieved initial results, there is currently no comprehensive regulatory framework that can be applied to various application scenarios.

This article studies the supervision of data on the consortium blockchain. With the current popularity of consortium blockchain technology, the amount of data is increasing on the consortium blockchain. But there is a problem in that the legality of the data cannot be guaranteed. The users may face the risk of illegal data. To address the above problems, this article proposes the following hierarchical processing scheme which is based on the regular expressions and smart contracts for the illegal data on the blockchain:

1. For the various types of data with little impact generated by different businesses, regular expressions are used to filter and intercept illegal data accessed by the user client. The regulatory authority sets the corresponding matching rules, and other users cannot set the rules.
2. For data whose types are basically fixed and important, a lightweight transaction mark blocking method is used to match illegal data. In the off-chain part of the supervision node, smart contracts are used to mark illegal data that is difficult to determine. This method mainly includes multiple business contracts, a control contract, and a permission contract. The control contract is used by the regulatory authority to mark illegal data and can be reused in multiple business contracts to achieve a lightweight effect. Users will not be able to access the marked data. The permission contract is mainly used for the management of the identity and address of the regulatory authority. Only authorized institutions can mark illegal data.

2   Related Works

The blockchain is derived from Bitcoin, and the difference from the traditional digital currency system is that transactions on the blockchain do not require the intervention of a third party. In practical applications, many unsolvable financial problems can be solved by blockchain [11]. Blockchain is mainly divided into public, consortium, and private blockchains. A consortium blockchain refers to a blockchain whose consensus process is controlled by preselected nodes. It is mainly used in B2B scenarios such as transactions, settlements, or clearing between institutions. The development of consortium blockchain is mainly focused on large-scale applications that need to use blockchain to empower economic construction. Therefore, the supervision of the consortium blockchain is a hotspot. The supervision of data on the consortium blockchain has become an important research topic in the future. The data on the consortium blockchain needs to take some measures to deal with illegal data which needs these regulatory requirements [6].

In recent years, many researchers have begun to focus on the regulation of blockchain. Their research results are used in scenarios combined with blockchain supervision [1]. For example, in the food supervision aspect, Tao et al. [18] proposed an on-chain supervision method by researching malicious nodes on the blockchain. The nodes are corrected and replaced in time if malicious supervisory nodes are found. In terms of central bank digital currency supervision, Sun et al. [17] proposed a CBDC (Central Bank Digital Currency) model named MBDC based on permission blockchain. The establishment and maintenance of the blockchain are through the central bank and commercial banks. Their model leverages a multi-blockchain architecture and ChainID to enhance scalability. They have provided strong supervision over the security of the entire model through the establishment of a data center and a supervisory layer. Regarding the intelligent logistics system, Fu and Zhu [7] proposed the application of blockchain to the intelligent logistics system in response to copper leakage and traceability issues in system supervision. The establishment of a variety of different "multi-authentication centers" for different events. The introduction of blockchain improves the efficiency of the operation of the smart logistics system and the supervision capabilities. In terms of e-government affairs, Lin et al. [13] proposed a strong supervision model of blockchain based on the threshold ring signature algorithm. This model can greatly control the error rate of blockchain information and improve the processing efficiency of e-government. The above-mentioned supervision schemes introduce the contents of supervision nodes and how to improve supervision capabilities. But none of these schemes involve solutions for dealing with the possible illegal data on the blockchain.

The concept of smart contract was proposed by cryptographer Nick Szabo, and the smart contract can be automatically executed when the corresponding conditions [4]. A smart contract is essentially a piece of executable code, which functions by being deployed on the blockchain. Yong et al. [21] proposed a "vaccine blockchain" system based on blockchain and machine learning. By designing appropriate smart contracts, the vaccine blockchain system can intelligently monitor the status of the system and provide query functions. Zhang et al. [23] proposed a framework based on smart contracts, in which the judge contract is used to judge bad behavior and return the corresponding punishment. Liu et al. [14] proposed a smart contract access control service scheme with lower cost than other access control rule frameworks. Khatoon [10] proposed a blockchain-based smart contract healthcare system. Their system uses smart contracts to record data. At the same time, different smart contracts are designed for different medical workflows, and they have access to data between different entities in the system. Although many people have proposed many framework models for access control through smart contracts. However, there are still few studies on the supervision of blockchain data through smart contract access control [22].

3   System Model and Design Goals

3.1   System Model

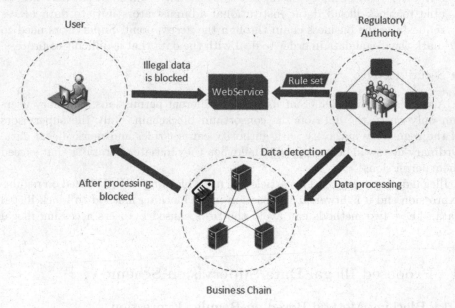

Fig. 1. System model

The system consists of three types of entities namely users, regulatory authority, and business chain which are shown in Fig. 1. Users need to initiate a request to the regulatory authority through the access point when they access data. The regulatory authority extracts the data on the business chain for detection. The data on the business chain will be processed if there is illegal data. And processed data will be blocked for users.

With the popularity of blockchain, the data capacity on the blockchain is constantly expanding. And data that violates laws are easy to appear on the blockchain, and information supervision on the blockchain has also become a difficult problem. However, these data cannot be viewed when the user sends a request [19]. So it is necessary to block the illegal data in time when the user sends these requests. In summary, in order to achieve a hierarchical processing scheme for illegal data on the blockchain, the design of the system must meet the following requirements.

- User level

1. Ordinary users: Ordinary users initiate data access requests to the business chain through the access point. Supervisors need to embed corresponding rules to filter and block data related to violations of laws and regulations. In the end, users cannot access the illegal data with little impact generated by different businesses.
2. Institutional administrators: As institutional administrators have greater authority than ordinary users, the rules set for ordinary users may not be able to block illegal data. Institutional administrators initiate data access requests to the business chain through the access point. Supervisors need to mark the illegal data in order to deal with the data that is difficult to process.

- Security level

1. Access permission: Different users have different permissions. Ordinary users can only query the data on the consortium blockchain. Only the supervisors of the regulatory authority with authority can set rules and mark illegal data. Ordinary users will be prompted to fail when they initiate operations that exceed their permissions.
2. Illegal data processing: This article will use a blocking method based on regular expression and a lightweight transaction mark blocking method to block illegal data. These two methods can avoid the risks caused by users accessing illegal data.

4   Proposed Illegal Data Supervision Scheme

4.1   Blocking Method Based on Regular Expression

The immutability of the blockchain makes it difficult to delete and modify the illegal data inserted into the business chain. As shown in Fig. 2, this article proposes a method for ordinary users to filter and block the data accessed by the user terminal based on regular expressions. When the user requests to access the data on the business chain, if the data is illegal, the request is rejected.

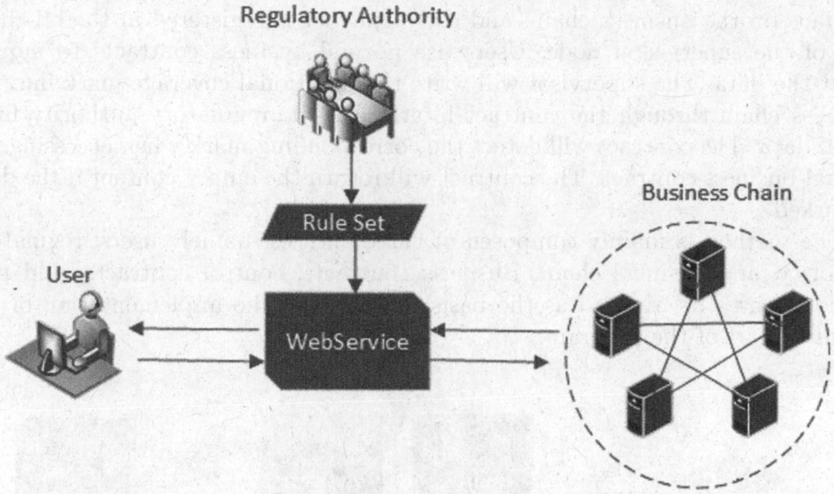

Fig. 2. Blocking method based on the regular expression

This method combines the requirements and characteristics of the actual business. The method sets illegal data access filters based on regular expressions at the user's access point. This method can flexibly change the matching rules and is suitable for quickly blocking illegal data. After filtering such illegal data, clients of the business chain will be restricted from accessing such resources. At the same time, the regulatory authority can set and deploy rules on the network server. First, the user needs to send a data request to the business chain through the webserver. Data returned by the business chain will be matched according to the rules deployed by the regulatory authorities. The data will be directly filtered out and users cannot access illegal data if it does not meet the requirements of the rules.

After the user enters the data that needs to be queried, the matched related data is sent to the user through the SDK. Illegal data need to be retrieved and replaced before the user receives the data. The illegal data will be replaced with * if the match is successful.

4.2   Lightweight Transaction Mark Blocking Method

The method targets users with greater authority such as institutions, units, or departments that own business chain nodes proposing a lightweight transaction mark blocking technology, which is shown in Fig. 3. Restricting access to illegal data on the chain can meet certain business needs. However, the disadvantage is that institutions, units, or departments that hold business chain nodes can still access illegal data. In summary, in the actual business scenarios, users and node-holding institutions need to be blocked on the side of data. Therefore, in response to such a demand, this solution proposes a lightweight transaction mark blocking method. This method deploys smart contracts with a unified operation interface on the business chain, and each contract is registered in the off-chain part of the supervision node. Users use normal business contracts to inquire about the data. The supervisor will write the additional coverage mark into the business chain through the contract interface if the regulatory authority finds illegal data. The contract will detect the corresponding mark when accessing the normal business contract. The contract will return the empty content if the data is marked.

The method is mainly composed of three entities, namely users, regulatory authority, and business chain. Business contracts, control contracts, and permission contracts are used as the basis to complete the implementation of the technical part of the program.

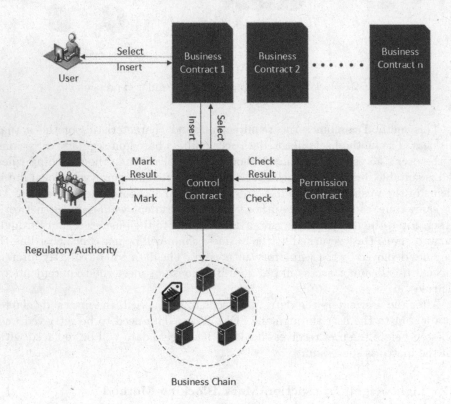

Fig. 3. Lightweight transaction mark blocking method flow chart

The control contract receives the data transmitted by the business contract, adds a field for marking at the end of the received data field, and sets the initial value of the marked field to 0. First, the control contract needs to determine whether the address of the user who initiated the change of the marked field is the address of the supervisor. The marked field can be updated if the address belongs to the permission table. The data can be queried normally if the field is marked with 0. It will return a null value if the field marked on the blockchain is 1. The specific algorithm is shown in Algorithm 1.

Algorithm 1: Lightweight transaction mark blocking method

Input: data from business contract
Output: result
1 add mark field when creating business table;
2 set the initial value of mark to 0;
3 the user makes a query;
4 the permission contract establishes a supervisor's address table;
5 **if** *data belongs to illegal* **then**
6 | transfer the adrress table from permission;
7 **end**
8 **if** *msg.sender is in table* **then**
9 | $1 \leftarrow mark$;
10 **else**
11 | the value of mark remains unchanged;
12 **end**
13 **foreach** *mark* **do**
14 | **if** *mark=0* **then**
15 | | return the data;
16 | **else**
17 | | determined as illegal data, return *;
18 | **end**
19 **end**

This article proposes three types of smart contract, including business contract, control contract, and permission contract. The business contract is used for users to insert data on the blockchain according to different business requirements. The control contract is used to mark illegal data on the blockchain. And the permission contract is used to manage the address of users who have the authority to control the control contract. The details of the three types of contracts and the use process of the contracts will be introduced in detail below.

- **Contract introduction**

1. Business contract: The business contract is called by the user, and multiple different business contracts can be written for different business requirements. The content of the business contract depends on actual requirements, such as specific table names, table fields, and functions. The actions involved in the contract mainly include inserting, selecting, deleting, updating, etc. The business contract needs to transmit data to the control contract. The function of the business contract is mainly to manage the data released by the user on the business chain.

2. Control contract: The control contract is called by the business contract. For multiple different business contracts, the control contract can be reused multiple times. The control contract provides an interface for the business contract to receive the data transmitted by the business contract to the control contract. After the control contract receives the table-building data of the business contract, it adds a mark field in the table. The main function of the control contract is to mark and block the data on the business chain. The mark field of illegal data will be updated from the initial value of 0 to 1 by the supervisor. The updated record is inserted into the business chain.

3. Permission contract: The permission contract is called by the control contract and is deployed by the regulatory authority. The function of the contract is to store the supervisor's address information in the permission table. An addrcode is set when the table is created, and the permissions corresponding to the address are set. Addrcode is used to store the supervisor's address information. It means there is no permission if the boolean value of addrcode is false. Otherwise, it means permission. In the permission contract, the address table can be inserted, selected, deleted, and updated. Only the person judged as the supervisor can call the function of updating the marked field in the control contract. Other unauthorized users cannot call the control contract to update the marked field.

The data needs to be marked if the data is illegal. The supervisor of the regulatory authority has the authority to mark illegal data. In the end, the illegal data after being marked cannot be queried by users. The supervisor does not need to make a mark and users can query this kind of data if the data is legal. The specific situation is shown in Table 1.

Table 1. Illegal data processing form

Data	Mark	Marker	Inquire
Violation	Yes	Supervisor	No
No violation	No	\	Yes

• **Specific process**

1. Inserting data into the business chain: The user calls the insert function of the business contract and transmits specific data to the control contract through the interface provided by the control contract. The control contract works by inserting data into the business chain and adding a field for marking before uploading the data to the business chain. The initial value of the marked field is set to 0. The regulatory authority initiates an update request to the marked field by calling the update mark field of the control contract. The control contract obtains the addrcode corresponding to the caller's address

by calling the update mark field. It means that there is no permission if the boolean value is false. Otherwise, there is permission. The supervisor in the regulatory authority can update the marked field if it is judged to be authorized.

2. User queries the data: The user queries a piece of data by calling the select function of the business contract. The business contract calls the select function of the control contract to query the data on the business chain. The value returned to the user is null if the value corresponding to the marked field of a piece of data on the business chain is 1. Finally, a lightweight transaction mark blocking method is realized.

5   Analysis and Comparison

5.1   Security Analysis

Theorem 1. *Different users have different permissions. Ordinary users can only query the data on the consortium blockchain. Only the supervisors of the regulatory authority with authority can set rules and mark illegal data. Ordinary users will be prompted to fail when they initiate actions that exceed their permissions.*

Proof. In the Solidity language, some global variables can be called by all functions. One of them is msg.sender, which refers to the address of the current caller or smart contract. In Solidity, function execution always needs to start from the external caller. A contract will only do nothing on the blockchain unless someone calls the function in it, so msg.sender always exists. The permission contract maintains a supervisor address information table. The msg.sender will obtain the real address of the current caller and match the data in the table to control access rights when a user initiates a marking request for data.

Theorem 2. *This article uses blocking methods based on regular expression and lightweight transaction mark blocking methods to block illegal data, which can avoid the risks caused by users accessing illegal data.*

Proof. For various types of data with little impact generated by different businesses, a blocking method based on regular expression is used to match illegal data. For data whose types are fixed and important, a lightweight transaction mark blocking method is used to match illegal data. These two methods are combined to realize the blocking of illegal data, and the final result is that the combined use of the two methods can prevent users from accessing the risk of illegal data. Neither ordinary users nor institutional administrators can access it.

5.2   Theoretical Analysis

As shown in Table 2, Chen et al. [3] proposed a blockchain-based payment collection system, which realizes supervision by storing transaction details in a cloud database. Sun et al. [17] used the multi-blockchain architecture and blockchain identification to improve the scalability of the model and process payments faster. Lin et al. [13] applied blockchain to e-government issues, and a strong supervision model of blockchain based on a threshold ring signature algorithm is proposed.

In this article, it is mainly achieved by using smart contracts to supervise illegal data. The author analyzes and compares the scheme with the solutions of Zhang et al. [23] that use smart contracts to implement access control. In their scheme, they proposed a framework based on smart contracts to implement distributed trusted access control for IoT systems. Multiple access control contracts are used to achieve access control between multiple subject-object pairs. Their scheme uses register contracts to manage access control methods such as register, update, delete methods, etc. But for objects that manage access control methods whether there are any risks associated with changes has not been specifically introduced. The permission contract part of our scheme registers all supervisor address users with supervisor authority into one address table. Only supervisors with authority can mark the illegal data in the control contract.

Table 2. Theoretical comparison

Scheme	Supervision method	Access control	Application scenarios
Chen et al.'s scheme [3]	Blockchain	\	Bitcoin collection
Sun et al.'s scheme [17]	Multi-blockchain and ChainID	\	Digital currency
Lin et al.'s scheme [13]	Threshold Ring Signature algorithm	\	e-government
Zhang et al.'s scheme [23]	Smart contracts	✓	IoT
This article	Regular expressions and smart contracts	✓	e-government,etc

5.3 Experiment Analysis

This article uses a computer configured with Intel(R) Core(TM) i5-7500 CPU @ 3.40GHz to build an Ubuntu 16.04 operating system environment for experimentation. The blockchain test network is carried out on the underlying platform of the FISCO BCOS blockchain. A FISCO BCOS with four peers and raft consensus is running on the platform. Through the establishment of nodes and node pre-service (WeBASE-Front) and the WeBASE-Front contract editor, the contract is edited, compiled, deployed, and debugged. The FISCO BCOS supports distributed storage, which enables storage to break through the limit of a single machine and supports horizontal expansion. In addition, the Java-based stress testing tool Apache JMeter developed by the Apache organization is used for the performance testing of smart contracts.

The blocking method based on regular expression is to set data access filtering based on regular expressions at the user access. The program uses the Apache

JMeter stress test tool to stress test the five interfaces of the program, and set different total sample numbers. The total number of samples is set to 1000, 1500, 2000, 2500, 3000, and other different numbers for testing. At the same time, the request interval is set to 1s. The experimental results are shown in Fig. 4.

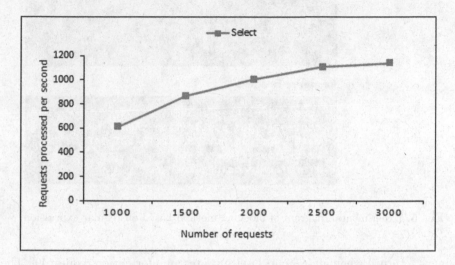

Fig. 4. Throughput of illegal data blocking method based on regular expression

The data query request initiated by the client will be synchronized on the blockchain. The data is first queried on the blockchain and then returned to the user through the SDK middleware. The author assumes that the test is an illegal vocabulary, and it needs to be blocked on the user side. The illegal data will be replaced with * if the word is contained on the blockchain. The experimental results are shown in Fig. 5.

In the lightweight transaction mark blocking method, we create an information table through a business contract to verify the effectiveness of the scheme. The interface from the control contract to the business contract is used to pass the data of the table to the control contract. The control contract is to add a marked field to the end of the data field in the table before the data is inserted into the business chain. The initial value is set to 0 to determine whether the record in the table is illegal data. After the control contract transmits the data to the business chain, the supervisor who has the right to update the marked field can update the marked field of the illegal data to 1 by operating the control contract. The supervisor needs to confirm the identity of the member when the supervisor calls the control contract to update the label field. The control contract uses the msg.sender method to determine the user address of the current calling contract and then calls the permission contract to confirm whether the address is in the permission table. The user can modify the marked field if the address is in the address table. The marked field of the data is 1 then a null

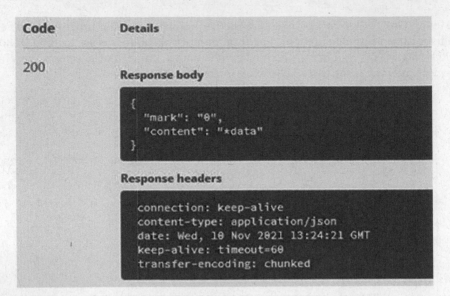

Fig. 5. Experimental diagram of blocking method based on regular expression

value is returned when an ordinary user initiates an information request [9]. The result of the transaction information marked by the supervisor on the data is shown in Fig. 6.

Apache JMeter tool to carry on performance tests to each method of a control contract, the test result is shown in Fig. 7. The Apache JMeter tool simulates five orders of magnitude requests sent by a user group. The throughput of the insert, update, and mark is similar, and stable between 100–300. The throughput of the select is between 600–800. The detailed performance data of the mark in the control contract is shown in Table 3. The data in the table includes the success rate of interface calls, the average transaction volume per second, and the average transaction response time.

Table 3. Detailed performance data of the marking method

Msamples	Ssuccess/%	Hmax/tps	Aaverage/tps	Trtt/s
1000	100	200	148.1	0.591
1500	100	300	189.4	0.660
2000	100	400	240.5	0.771
2500	100	400	231.2	0.842
3000	100	400	248.8	1.002

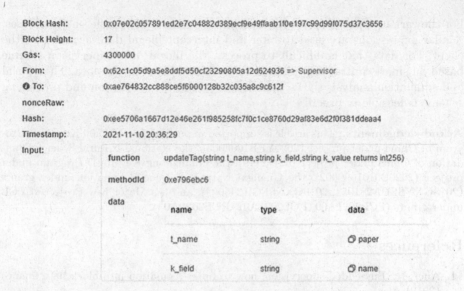

Fig. 6. Transaction information of lightweight transaction marking and blocking method

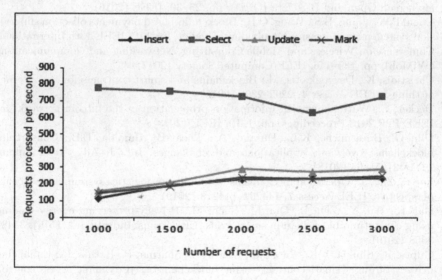

Fig. 7. Throughput of lightweight transaction mark blocking method

6 Conclusion

User access to illegal data on the consortium blockchain will bring serious problems. Our scheme proposes a solution for the supervision of illegal data on the blockchain. The illegal data blocking method based on regular expression and smart contracts, a grading solution for illegal data on the blockchain is proposed.

For the various types of data with little impact generated by different businesses, regular expressions are used to filter and intercept illegal data accessed by the client. For data that is difficult to process, the illegal data supervision scheme based on smart contracts is adopted to mark and block illegal data. Theoretical and simulation analysis shows that the illegal data classification and processing scheme is feasible in practice.

Acknowledgements. This article is supported in part by the National Key R&D Program of China under project (2020YFB1006003), the National Natural Science Foundation of China under project (62172119), the Guangdong Key R&D Program under project (2020B0101090002), the Guangxi Natural Science Foundation under grants (2018GXNSFDA281054, 2019GXNSFGA245004), and the Major Key Project of PCL under grants (PCL2021A09, PCL2021A02, PCL2022A03).

References

1. Auer, R.: Embedded supervision: how to build regulation into blockchain finance (2019)
2. Azaria, A., Ekblaw, A., Vieira, T., Lippman, A.: MedRec: using blockchain for medical data access and permission management. In: 2016 2nd International Conference on Open and Big Data (OBD), pp. 25–30. IEEE (2016)
3. Chen, P.W., Jiang, B.S., Wang, C.H.: Blockchain-based payment collection supervision system using pervasive bitcoin digital wallet. In: 2017 IEEE 13th International Conference on Wireless and Mobile Computing, Networking and Communications (WiMob), pp. 139–146. IEEE Computer Society (2017)
4. Christidis, K., Devetsikiotis, M.: Blockchains and smart contracts for the internet of things. IEEE Access **4**, 2292–2303 (2016)
5. Decker, C., Wattenhofer, R.: Information propagation in the bitcoin network. In: IEEE P2P 2013 Proceedings, pp. 1–10. IEEE (2013)
6. Dib, O., Brousmiche, K.L., Durand, A., Thea, E., Hamida, E.B.: Consortium blockchains: overview, applications and challenges. Int. J. Adv. Telecommun. **11**(1&2), 51–64 (2018)
7. Fu, Y., Zhu, J.: Operation mechanisms for intelligent logistics system: a blockchain perspective. IEEE Access **7**, 144202–144213 (2019)
8. Gai, K., Wu, Y., Zhu, L., Qiu, M., Shen, M.: Privacy-preserving energy trading using consortium blockchain in smart grid. IEEE Trans. Industr. Inf. **15**(6), 3548–3558 (2019)
9. Gupta, R., Shukla, V.K., Rao, S.S., Anwar, S., Sharma, P., Bathla, R.: Enhancing privacy through "smart contract" using blockchain-based dynamic access control. In: 2020 International Conference on Computation, Automation and Knowledge Management (ICCAKM), pp. 338–343. IEEE (2020)
10. Khatoon, A.: A blockchain-based smart contract system for healthcare management. Electronics **9**(1), 94 (2020)
11. Li, K., Li, H., Hou, H., Li, K., Chen, Y.: Proof of vote: a high-performance consensus protocol based on vote mechanism & consortium blockchain. In: 2017 IEEE 19th International Conference on High Performance Computing and Communications; IEEE 15th International Conference on Smart City; IEEE 3rd International Conference on Data Science and Systems (HPCC/SmartCity/DSS), pp. 466–473. IEEE (2017)

12. Li, Z., Kang, J., Yu, R., Ye, D., Deng, Q., Zhang, Y.: Consortium blockchain for secure energy trading in industrial internet of things. IEEE Trans. Industr. Inf. **14**(8), 3690–3700 (2017)
13. Lin, S., Li, J., Liang, W.: Research on strong supervision algorithm model based on blockchain in e-government. In: 2020 IEEE 5th Information Technology and Mechatronics Engineering Conference (ITOEC), pp. 345–349. IEEE (2020)
14. Liu, B., Sun, S., Szalachowski, P.: SMACS: smart contract access control service. In: 2020 50th Annual IEEE/IFIP International Conference on Dependable Systems and Networks (DSN), pp. 221–232. IEEE (2020)
15. Nakamoto, S.: Bitcoin: a peer-to-peer electronic cash system. Decentralized Bus. Rev. 21260 (2008)
16. Ouyang, L., Wang, S., Yuan, Y., Ni, X., Wang, F.: Smart contracts: architecture and research progresses. Acta Automatica Sinica **45**(3), 445–457 (2019)
17. Sun, H., Mao, H., Bai, X., Chen, Z., Hu, K., Yu, W.: Multi-blockchain model for central bank digital currency. In: 2017 18th International Conference on Parallel and Distributed Computing, Applications and Technologies (PDCAT), pp. 360–367. IEEE (2017)
18. Tao, Q., Cui, X., Huang, X., Leigh, A.M., Gu, H.: Food safety supervision system based on hierarchical multi-domain blockchain network. IEEE Access **7**, 51817–51826 (2019)
19. Wang, H., Wang, Y., Cao, Z., Li, Z., Xiong, G.: An overview of blockchain security analysis. In: Yun, X., et al. (eds.) CNCERT 2018. CCIS, vol. 970, pp. 55–72. Springer, Singapore (2019). https://doi.org/10.1007/978-981-13-6621-5_5
20. Wang, J., Li, L., Yan, Y., Zhao, W., Xu, Y.: Security incidents and solutions of blockchain technology application. Comput. Sci. **45**, 352–355 (2018)
21. Yong, B., Shen, J., Liu, X., Li, F., Chen, H., Zhou, Q.: An intelligent blockchain-based system for safe vaccine supply and supervision. Int. J. Inf. Manag. **52**, 102024 (2020)
22. Zgraggen, R.R.: Cyber security supervision in the insurance sector: smart contracts and chosen issues. In: 2019 International Conference on Cyber Security and Protection of Digital Services (Cyber Security), pp. 1–4. IEEE (2019)
23. Zhang, Y., Kasahara, S., Shen, Y., Jiang, X., Wan, J.: Smart contract-based access control for the internet of things. IEEE Internet Things J. **6**(2), 1594–1605 (2018)
24. Zheng, Z., Xie, S., Dai, H., Chen, X., Wang, H.: An overview of blockchain technology: architecture, consensus, and future trends. In: 2017 IEEE International Congress on Big Data (BigData Congress), pp. 557–564. IEEE (2017)
25. Zhu, L.H., et al.: Survey on privacy preserving techniques for blockchain technology. J. Comput. Res. Dev. **54**(10), 2170–2186 (2017)

Author Index

Printed in the United States
by Baker & Taylor Publisher Services